Transcribed SCORES

NICKEL nickel cr

Music transcriptions by Pete Billmann and Joel Dennis

ISBN 0-634-05166-0

HAL•LEONARD®
CORPORATION
7777 W. BLUEMOUND RD. P.O. BOX 13819 MILWAUKEE, WI 53213

Visit Hal Leonard Online at
www.halleonard.com

Ode to a Butterfly

Words and Music by Chris Thile

Gtr. 1: Capo II

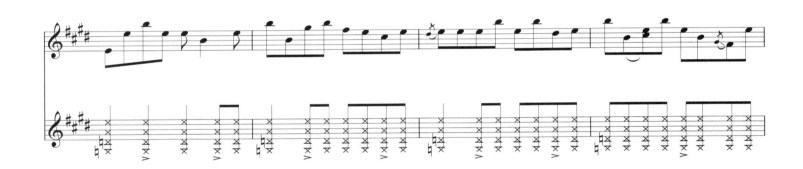

C

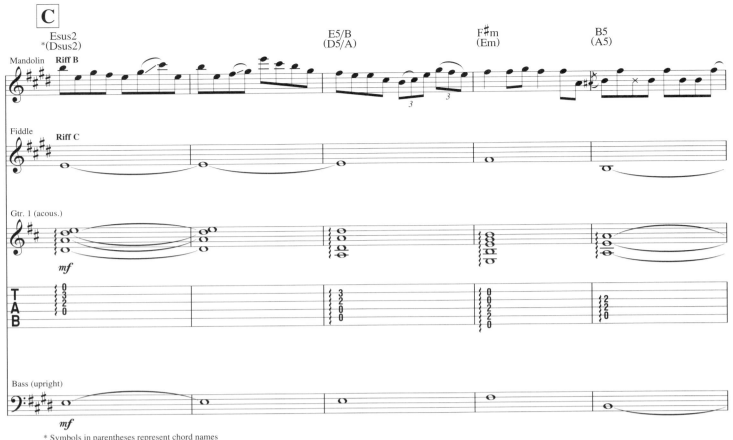

* Symbols in parentheses represent chord names
respective to capoed guitar. Symbols above reflect
actual sounding chords. Capoed fret is "0" in tab.

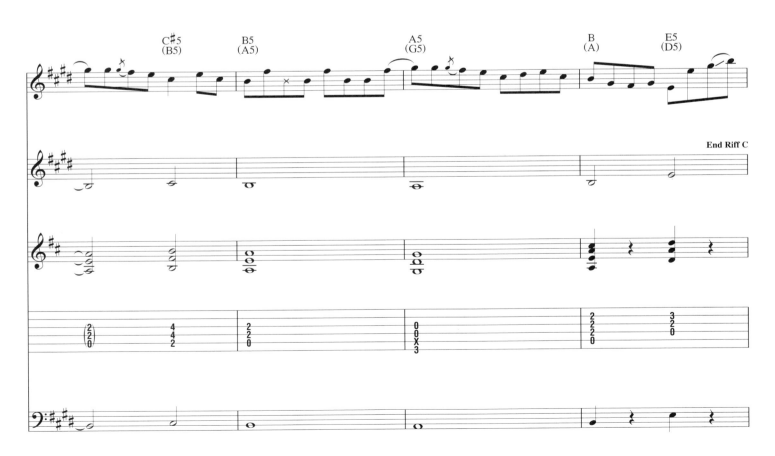

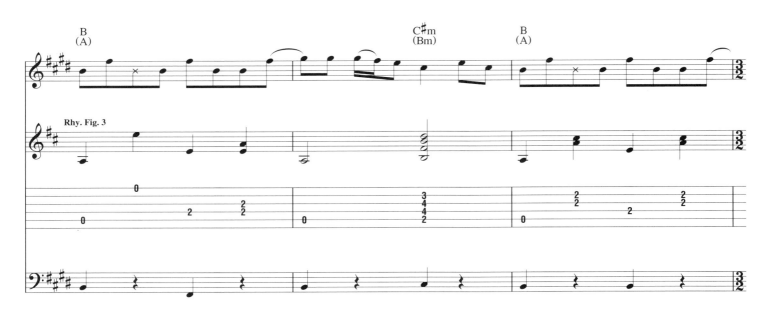

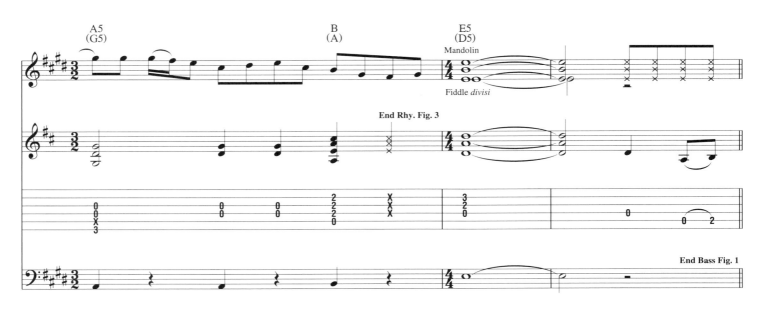

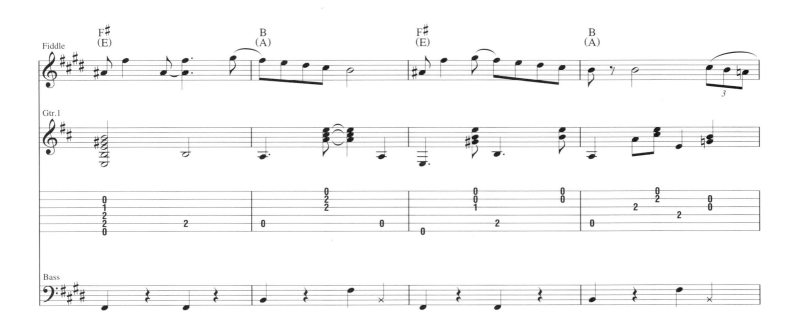

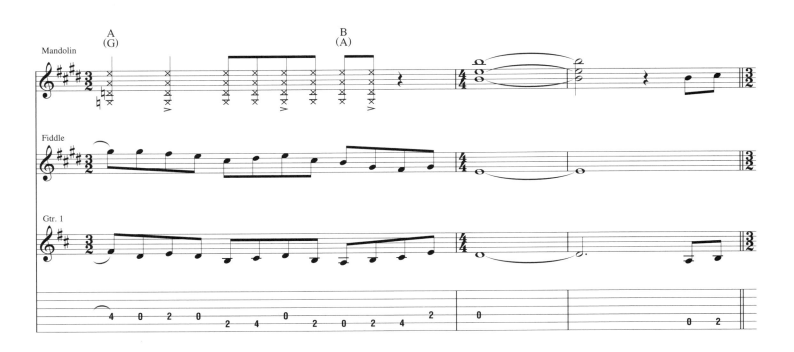

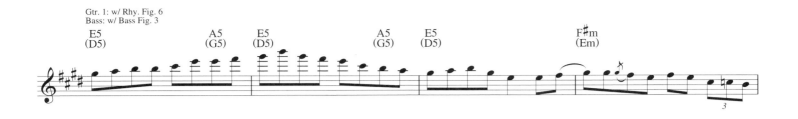

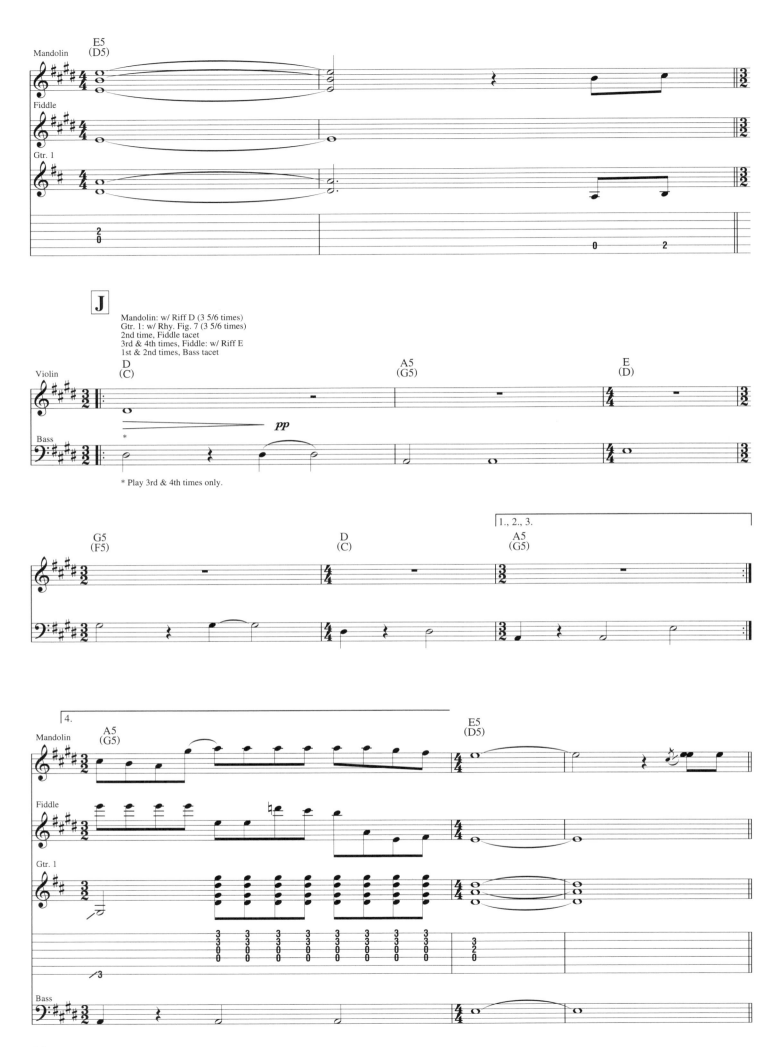

K

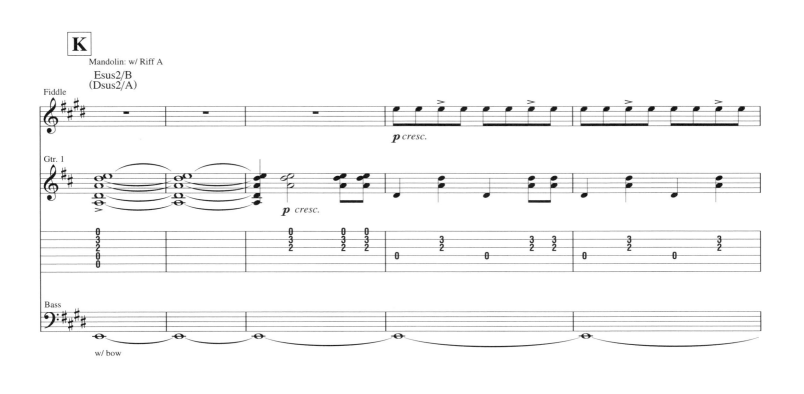

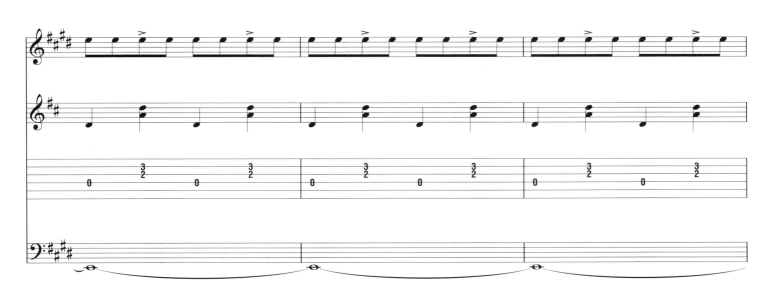

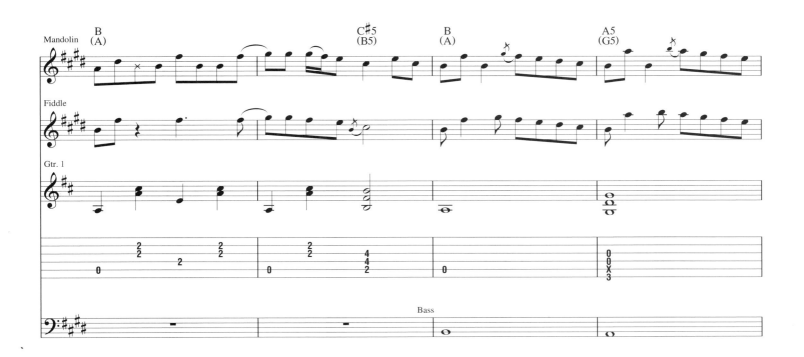

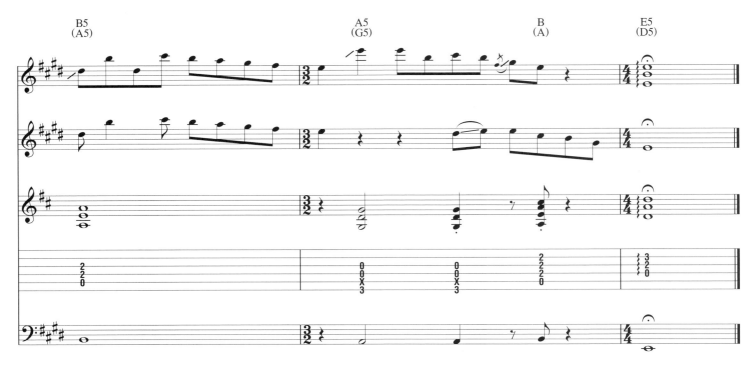

The Lighthouse's Tale

Words and Music by Adam McKenzie and Chris Thile

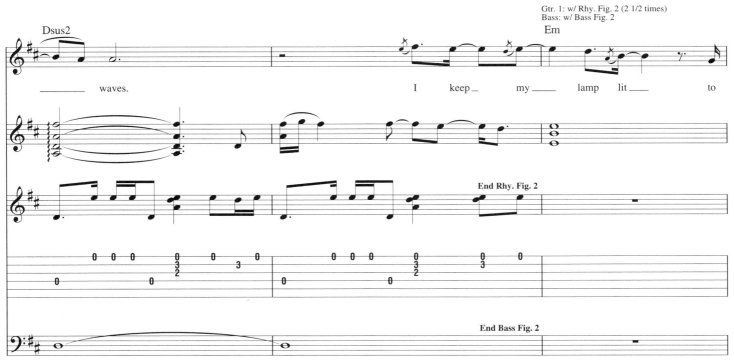

crash - ing a - round ___ me, and the sand ___ slips out ___ to ___

___ sea, and the ___ winds ___ that blow ___ re - mind ___ me ___ of what has been ___

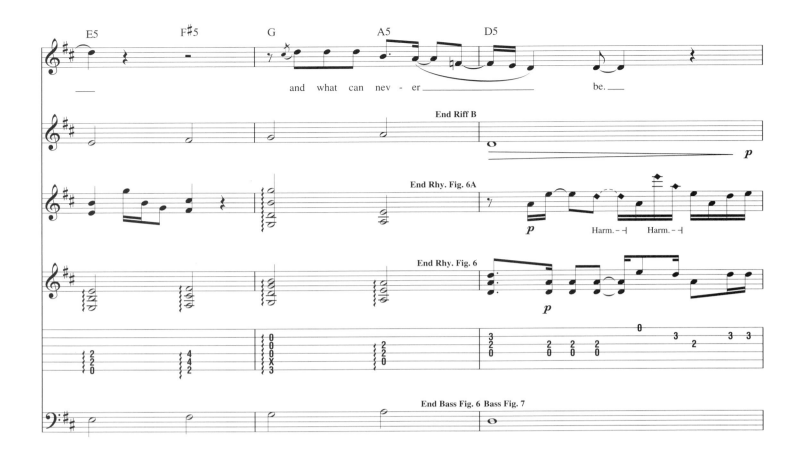

and what can nev - er _____ be. ___

End Riff B

End Rhy. Fig. 6A

Harm.─┤ Harm.─┤

End Rhy. Fig. 6

End Bass Fig. 6 Bass Fig. 7

Interlude
Gtr. 1: w/ Rhy. Fig. 1 (2 times)
Bass: w/ Bass Fig. 3 (1 1/2 times)

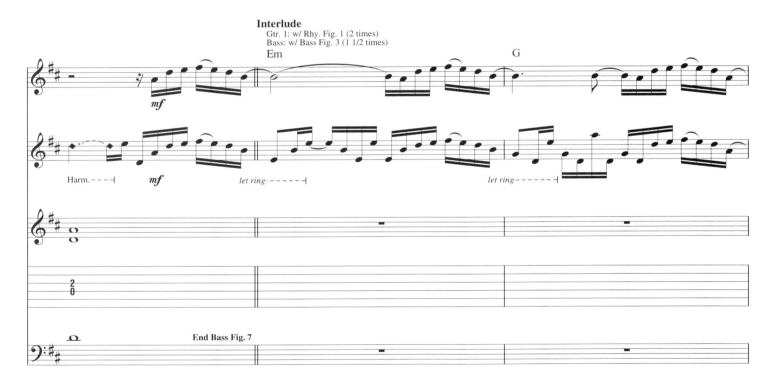

Harm.─ ─ ─ ─┤   *mf*   *let ring* ─ ─ ─ ─ ─┤   *let ring* ─ ─ ─ ─ ─┤

End Bass Fig. 7

Fiddle 1

Mandolin

let ring ─ ─ ─ ─ ─ ─ ─ ─┤   *let ring* ─

swore.   I saw him

cry - ing, ___ watched as ___ he bur - ried her in the ___ sand.

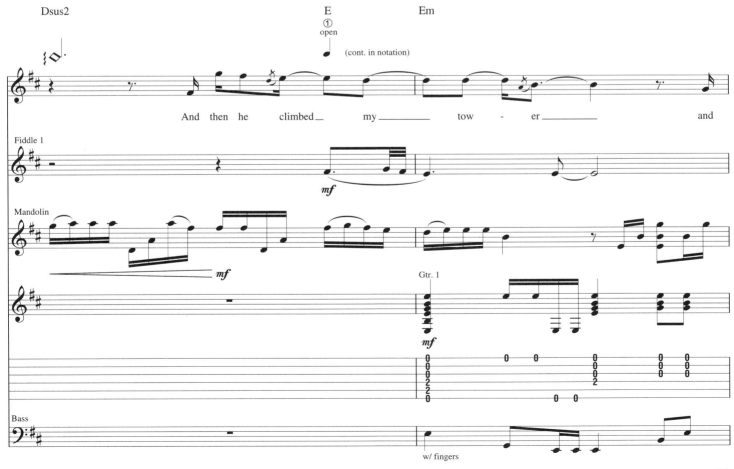

And then he climbed ___ my ___ tow - er ___ and

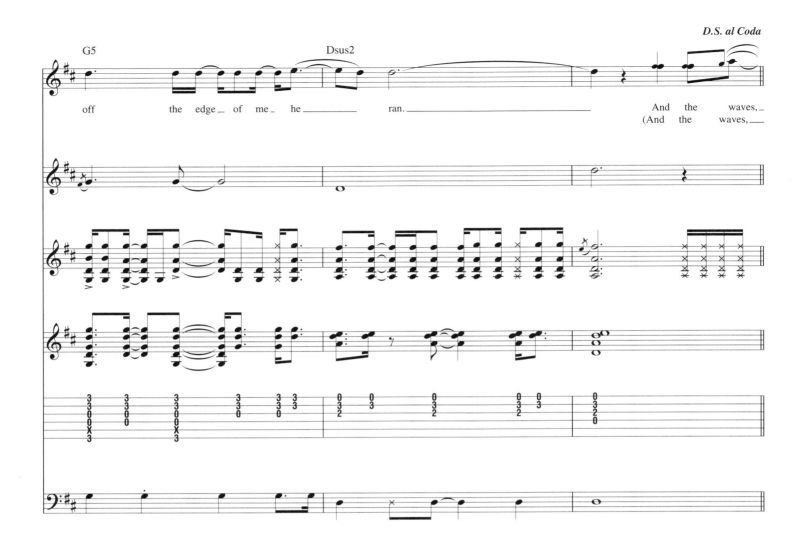

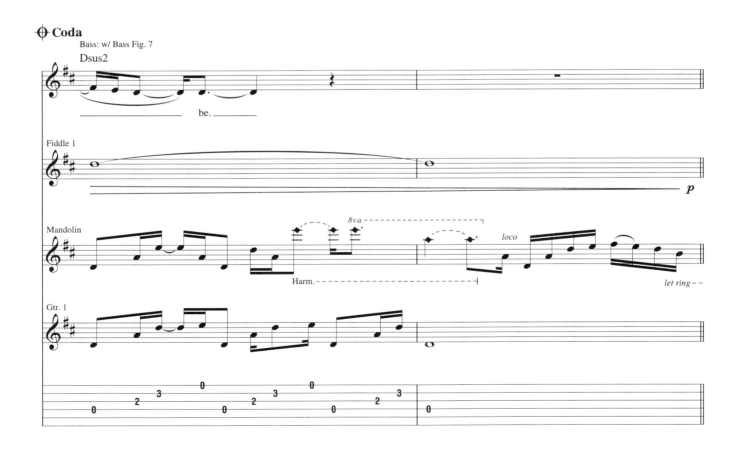

Interlude

Fiddle 1 tacet
Mandolin: w/ Riff A (last 4 meas.)
Gtr. 1: w/ Rhy. Fig. 1

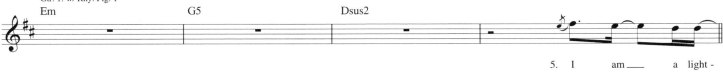

5. I am___ a light -

Verse

Gtr. 1: w/ Riff C (1 1/2 times)

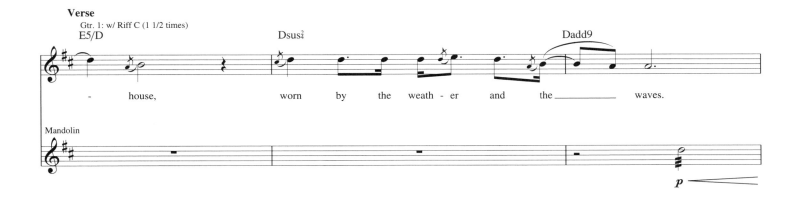

- house, worn by the weath - er and the _____ waves.

Mandolin

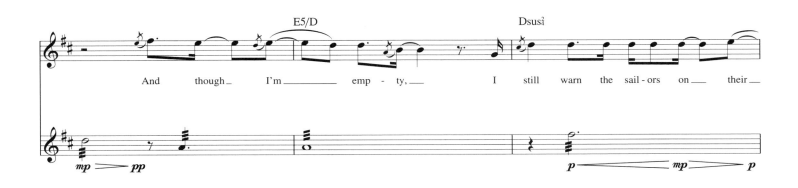

And though__ I'm_____ emp - ty, I still warn the sail - ors on__ their__

Mandolin tacet

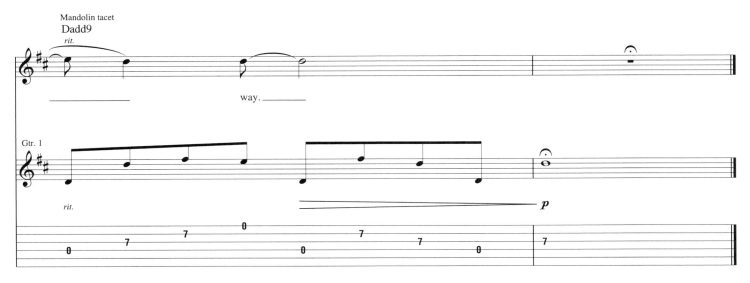

way._____

Gtr. 1

Out of the Woods

Words and Music by Sinead Lohan

Gtr. 1: DADGAD tuning:
(low to high) D-A-D-G-A-D
Bass: Drop D tuning:
(low to high) D-A-D-G
Bouzouki tuning:
(low to high) G-D-A-E

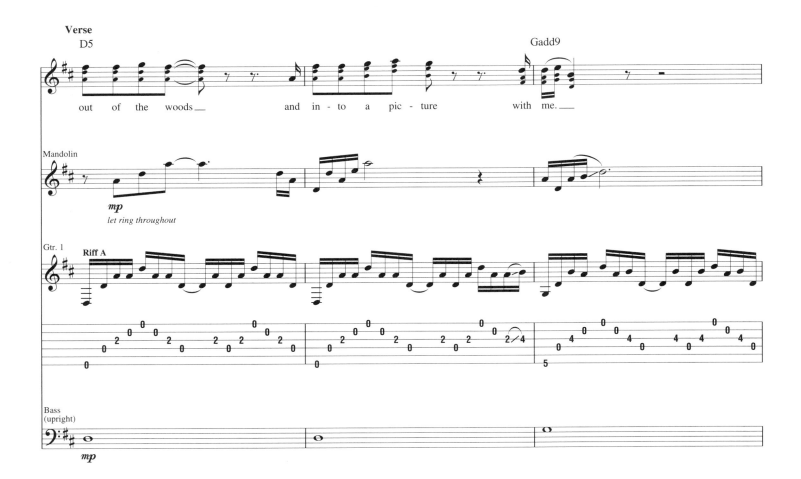

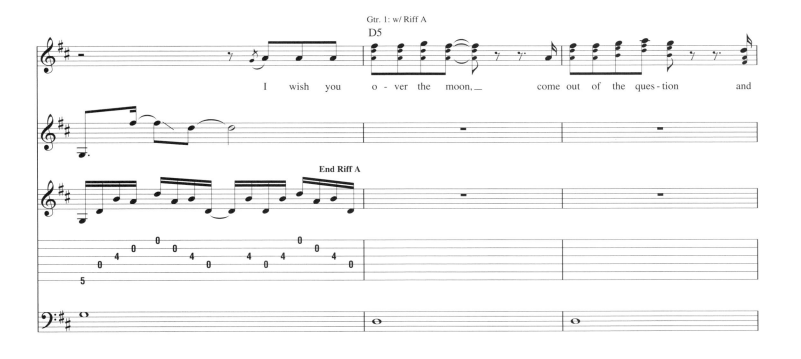

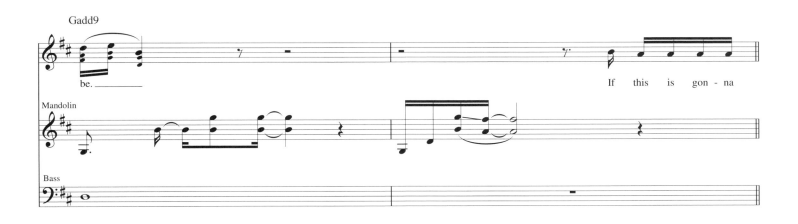

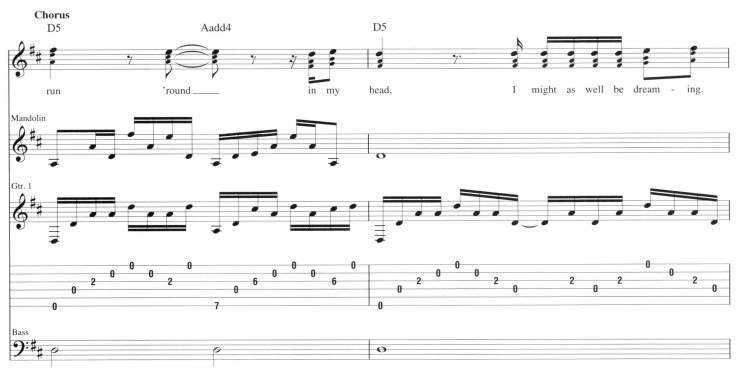

just like my heart ___ said it was gon-na be.   If this is gon-na

Chorus

run   'round ___   in my   head,   I might as well be dream-ing.   Run   'round ___   in my

Mandolin **Rhy. Fig. 2**

Gtr. 1 **Riff B**

Bass

Fiddle Solo
Mandolin: w/ Rhy. Fig. 1 (2 times)
Gtr. 1: w/ Riff A (2 times)

head.

Fiddle

Mandolin   **End Rhy. Fig. 2**

Gtr. 1   **End Riff B**

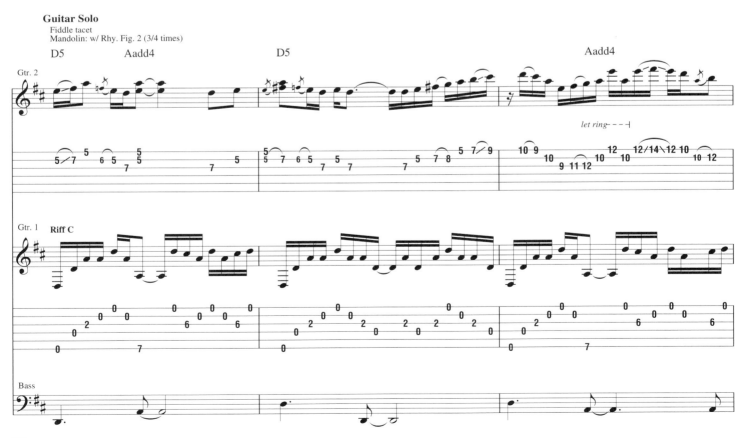

be. _____

If this is gon - na

Chorus

Fiddle tacet
Mandolin: w/ Rhy. Fig. 2 (2 times)
Gtr. 1: w/ Riff C (2 times)

run 'round ___ in my head, I might as well be dream - ing. Run 'round ___ in my

head. If this is gon - na run 'round ___ in my head, I might as well be dream - ing.

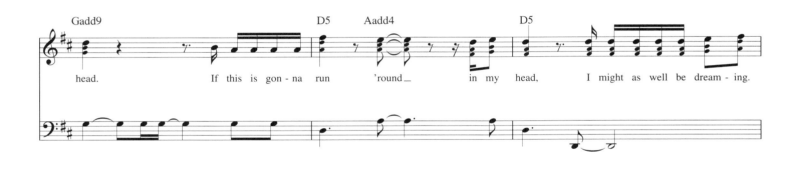

Run 'round ___ in my head, I might as well be dream - ing.
(Head.)

(Oo, _____

(I wish you

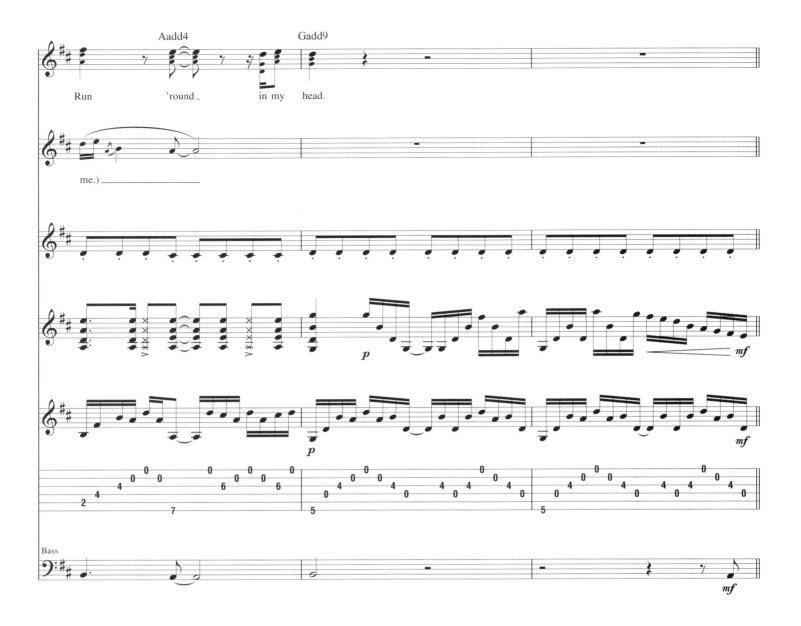

Outro
Gtr. 1: w/ Riff A (till fade)
Fiddle tacet
Bass: w/ Bass Fig. 1 (till fade)

In the House of Tom Bombadil

Words and Music by Chris Thile

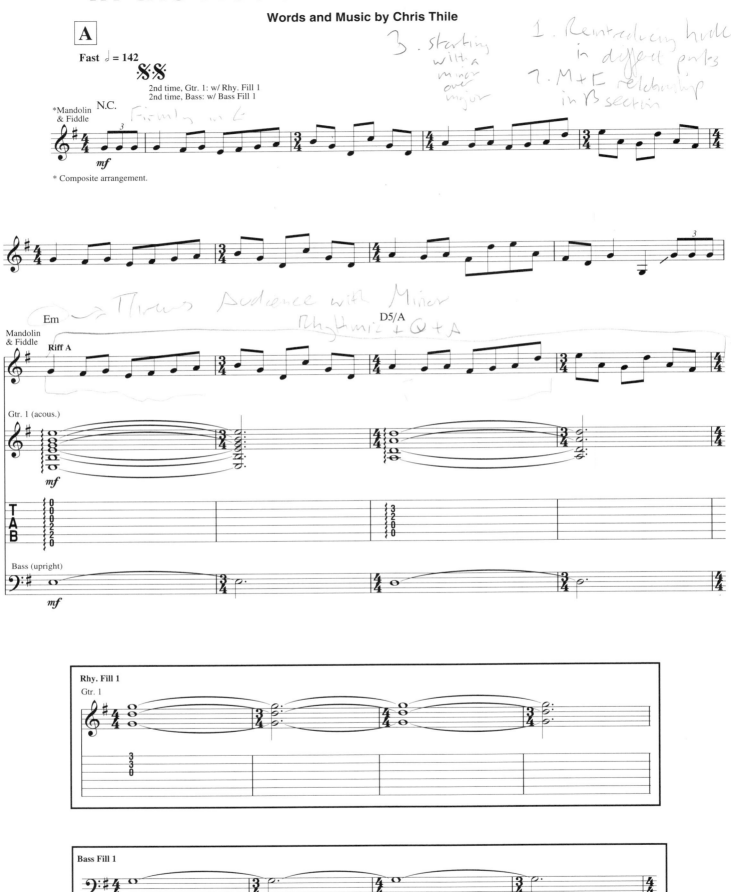

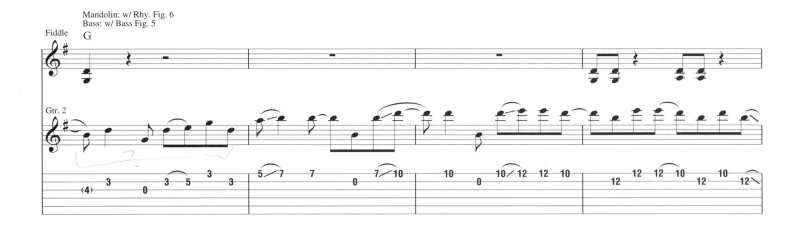

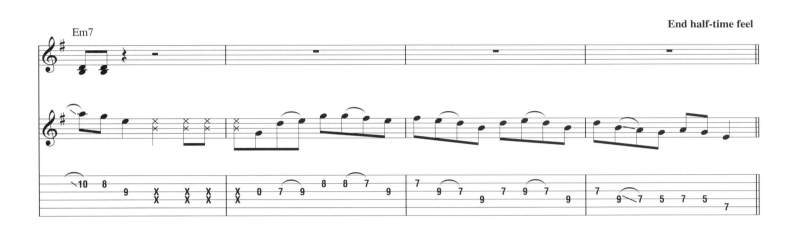

50

Fiddle

G5

Fiddle tacet

pp

Mandolin

Riff F

Gtr. 1

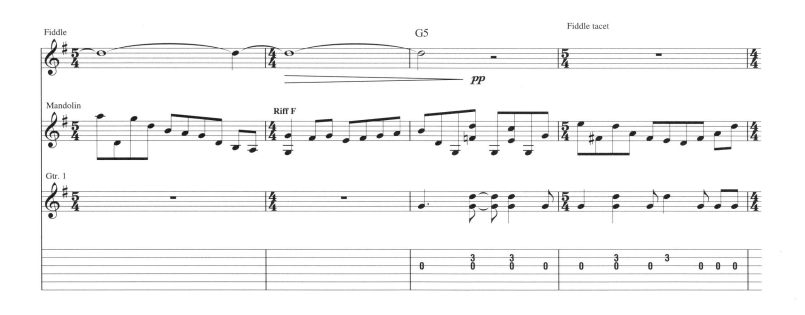

Mandolin

Gtr. 1

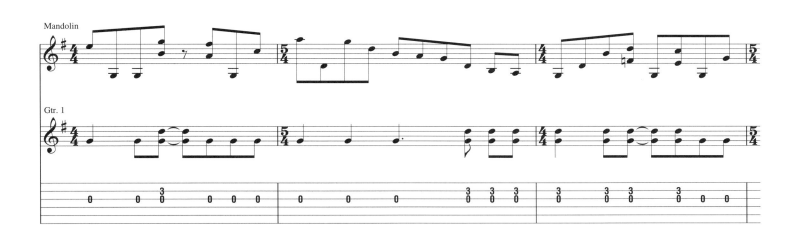

End Riff F

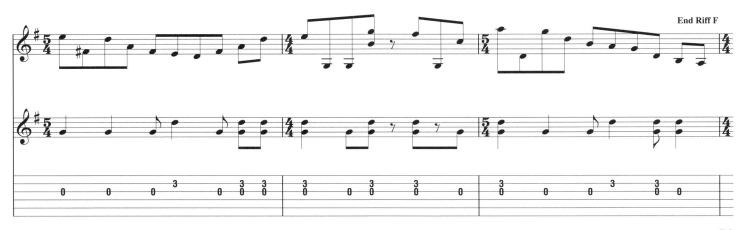

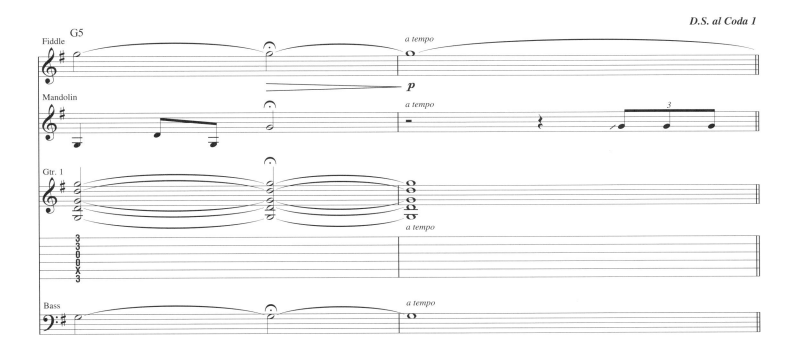

Reasons Why

Words and Music by Sean Watkins and David Puckett

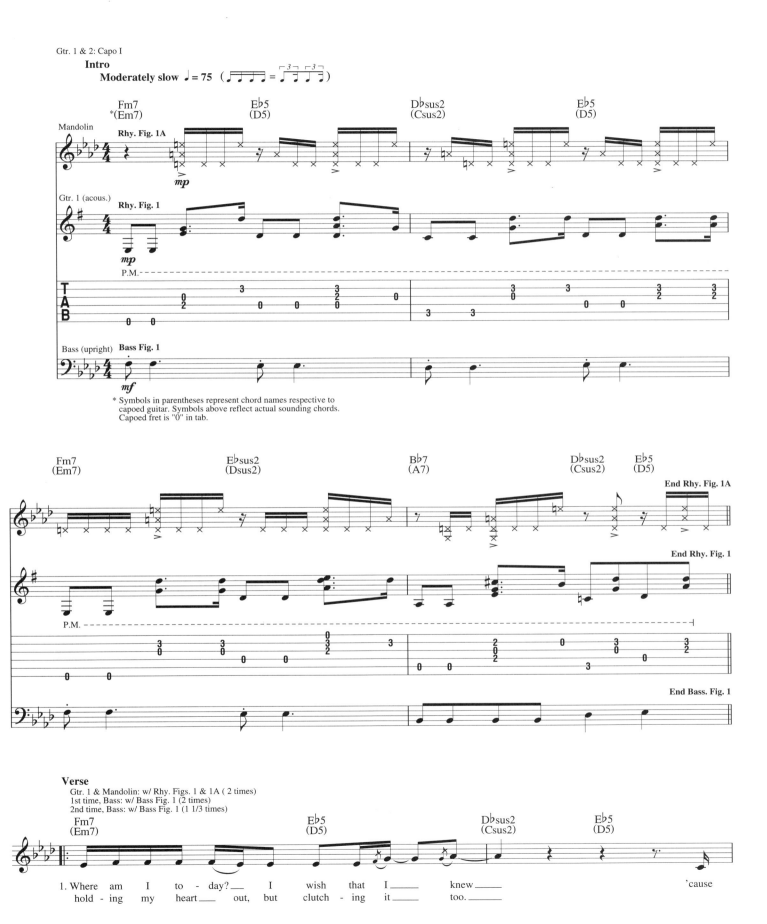

* Symbols in parentheses represent chord names respective to
capoed guitar. Symbols above reflect actual sounding chords.
Capoed fret is "0" in tab.

Verse

1. Where am I to-day?___ I wish that I knew ___ 'cause
hold-ing my heart ___ out, but clutch-ing it too.

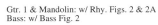

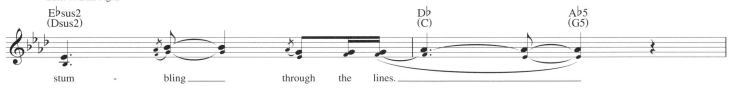

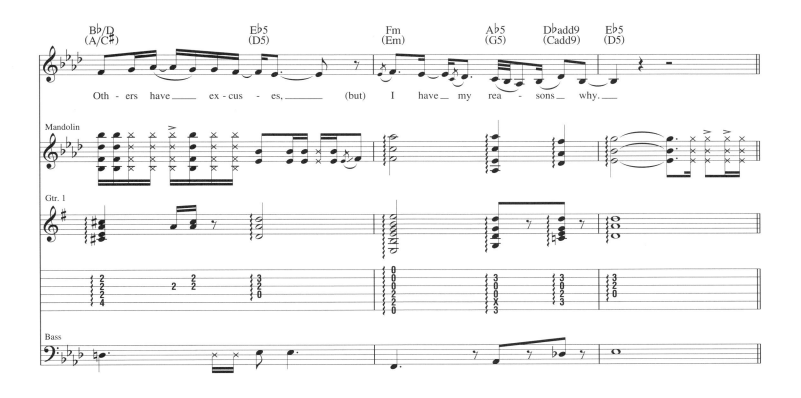

Guitar Solo

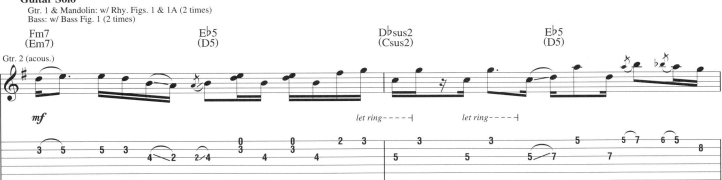

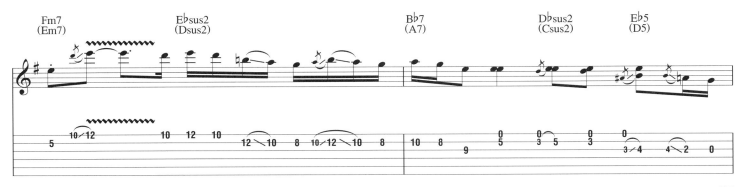

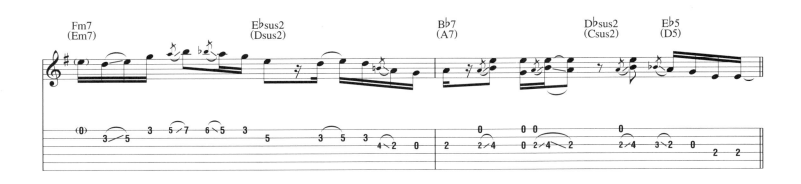

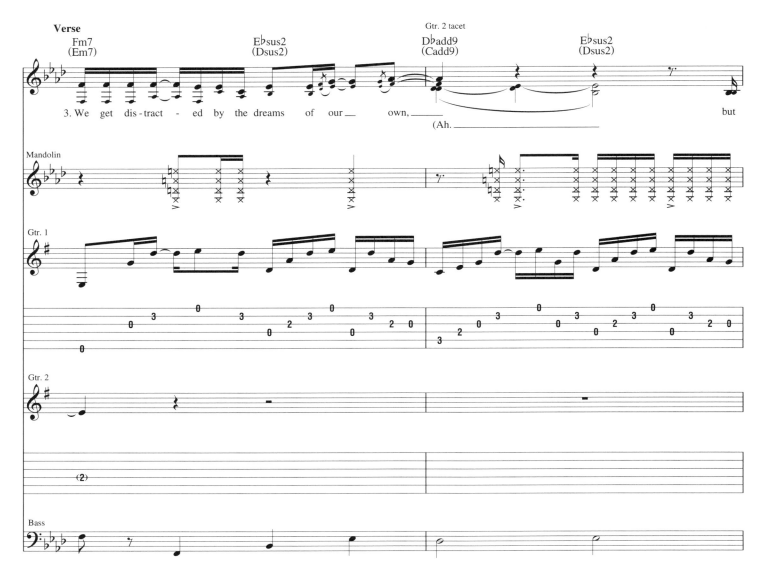

3. We get dis-tract-ed by the dreams of our own, but
(Ah.

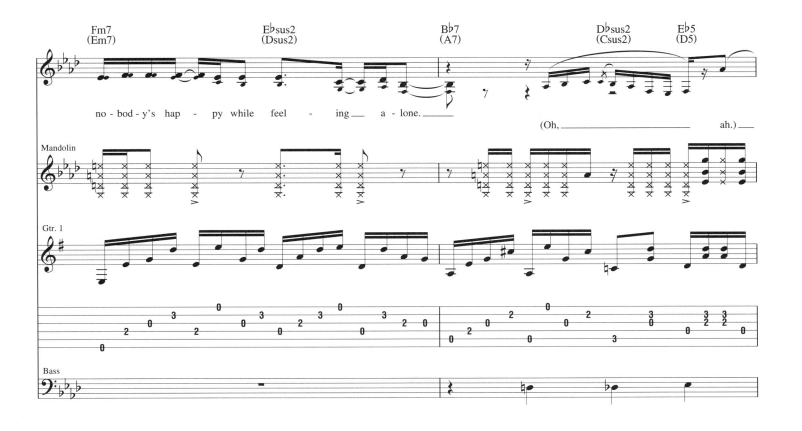

no - bod - y's hap - py while feel - ing _ a - lone. _____ (Oh, _____ ah.) _____

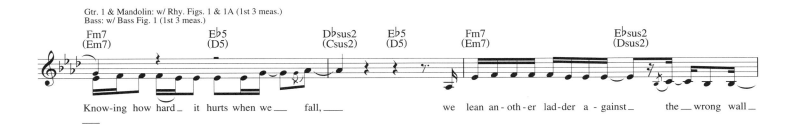

Gtr. 1 & Mandolin: w/ Rhy. Figs. 1 & 1A (1st 3 meas.)
Bass: w/ Bass Fig. 1 (1st 3 meas.)

Know-ing how hard _ it hurts when we _ fall, _____ we lean an-oth-er lad-der a-gainst _ the _ wrong wall _____

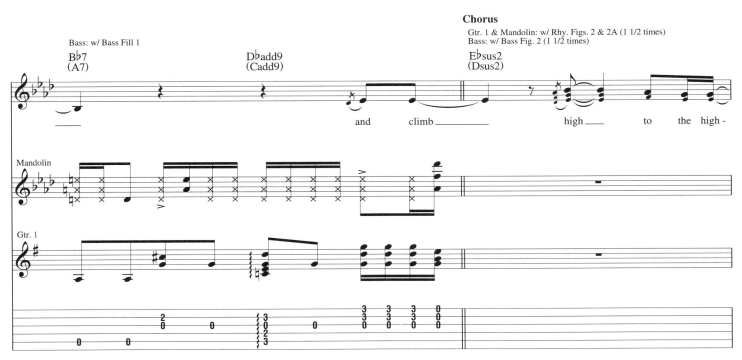

Chorus

Gtr. 1 & Mandolin: w/ Rhy. Figs. 2 & 2A (1 1/2 times)
Bass: w/ Bass Fig. 2 (1 1/2 times)

Bass: w/ Bass Fill 1

and climb _____ high _____ to the high -

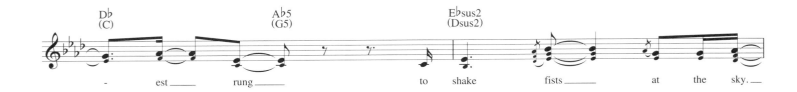

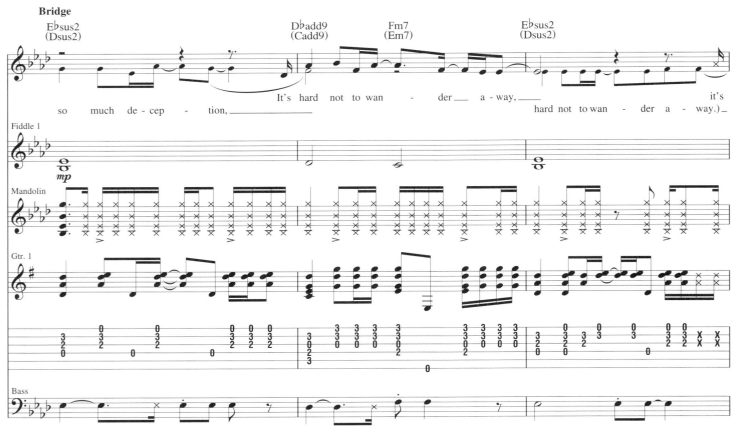

hard not to wan - der a - way.

When You Come Back Down

Words and Music by Danny O'Keefe and Tim O'Brien

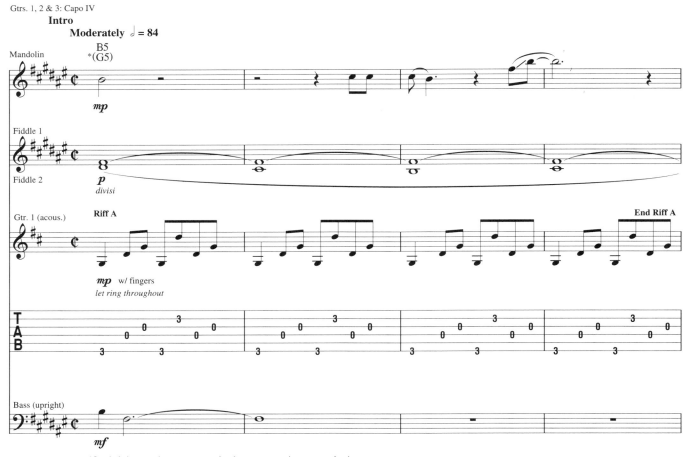

*Symbols in parentheses represent chord names respective to capoed guitar.
Symbols above reflect actual sounding chords. Capoed fret is "0" in tab.

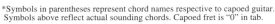

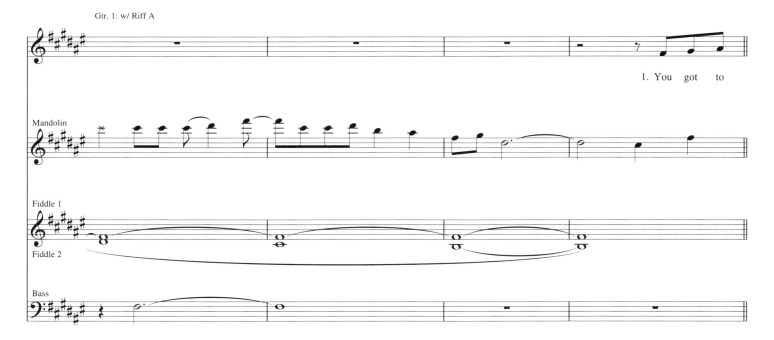

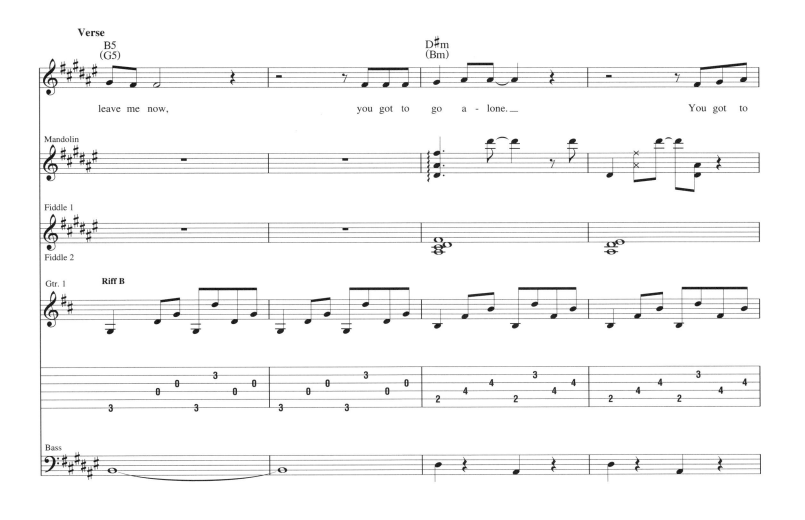

leave me now, you got to go a - lone._ You got to

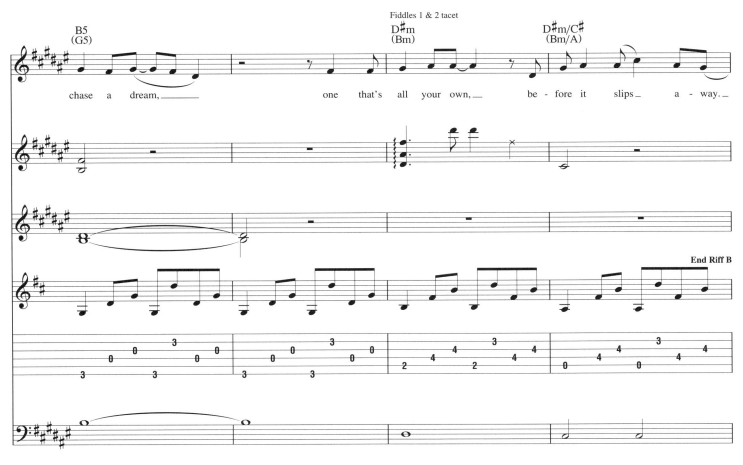

chase a dream,_ one that's all your own,_ be - fore it slips_ a - way._

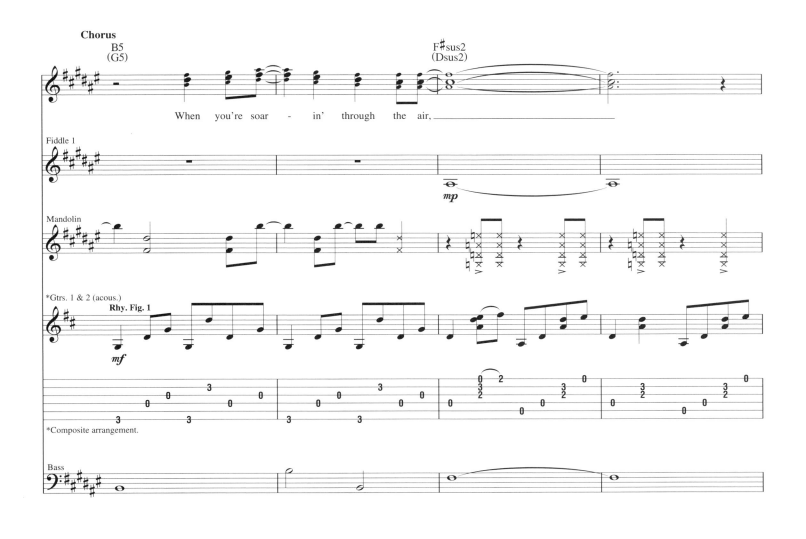

When you're soar - in' through the air,

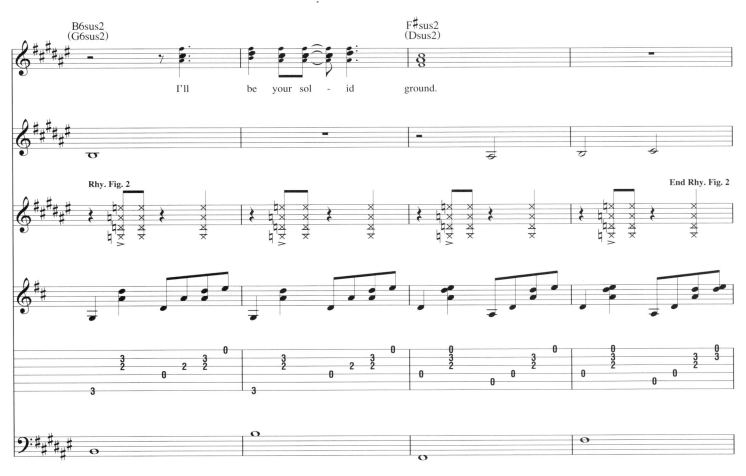

I'll be your sol - id ground.

Interlude

(I'll) catch you when ___ you fall.

Interlude

Your

Chorus

Mandolin: w/ Rhy. Fig. 2 (3 times)
Gtrs. 1 & 2: w/ Rhy. Fig. 1 (last 14 meas.)
Bass: w/ Bass Fig. 3 (2 times)

When you're soar - in' through the air, _____

I'll _____ be your sol - id ground.

Take ev - 'ry chance _ you dare. _____ I'll _ still be there _____

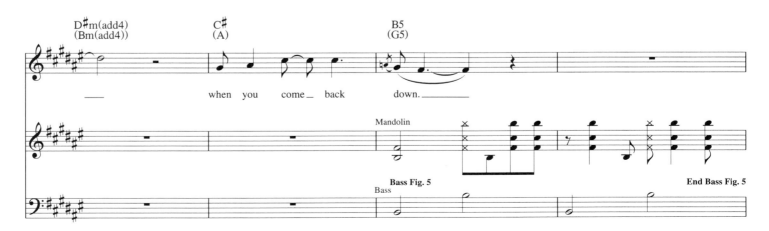

_____ when you come _ back down. _____

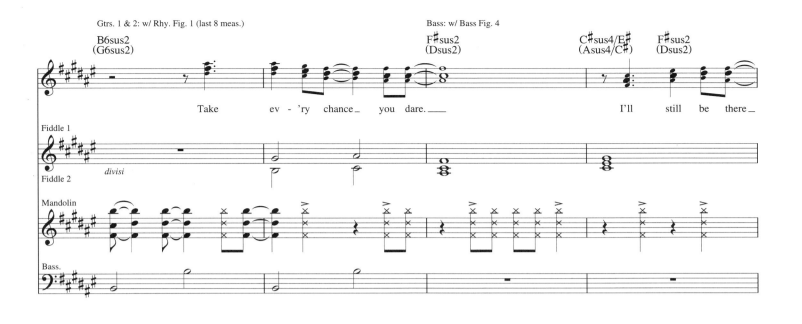

Take ev - 'ry chance___ you dare.___   I'll still be there___

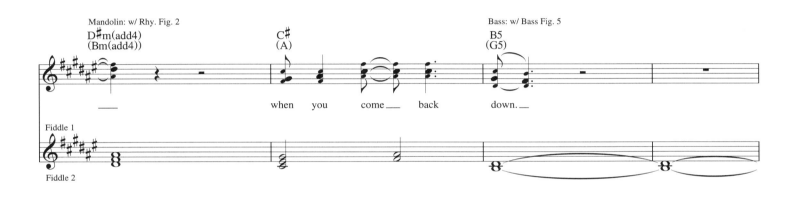

when you come___ back down.___

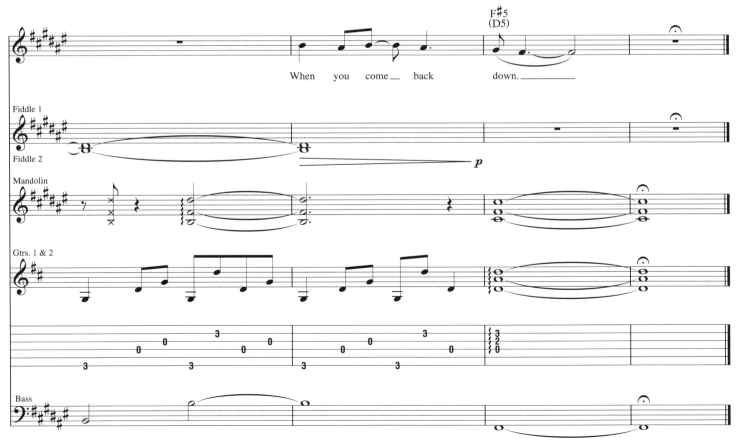

When you come___ back down._____

Sweet Afton

Lyrics by Robert Burns
Music by Chris Thile

Bouzouki tuning:
(low to high) G-D-A-E

song in thy praise._____ My

End Rhy Fig. 1A

End Rhy Fig. 1

Gtr. 1 & Mandolin: w/ Rhy. Figs. 1 & 1A

Badd4   Aadd9   E5

Mar - y's   a - sleep_____   by   thy   mur - mur - ing_____   stream.

C#m7   Badd4

Flow   gent - ly,   sweet_____   Af - ton,   dis -

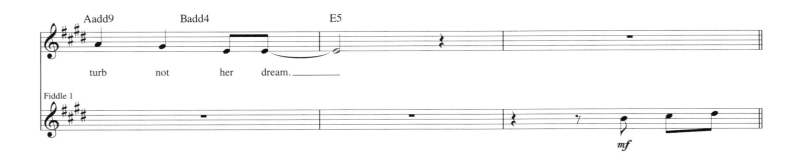

Aadd9   Badd4   E5

turb   not   her   dream._____

Fiddle 1

mf

Interlude

Mandolin: w/ Riff A
Fiddle 1: w/ Riff B

Gtr. 1: w/ Rhy. Fig. 1 (last 8 meas.)

E5   Aadd9   E5

Gtr. 1

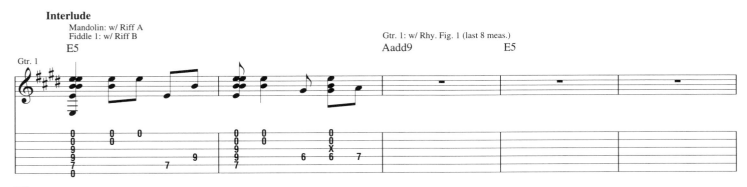

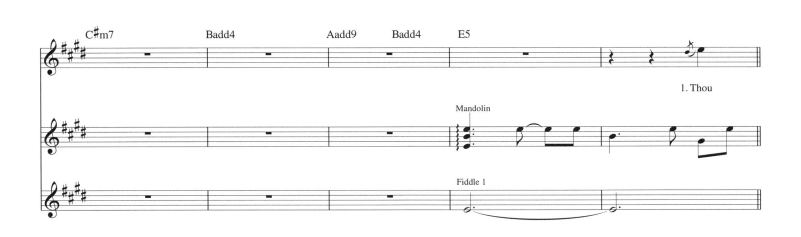

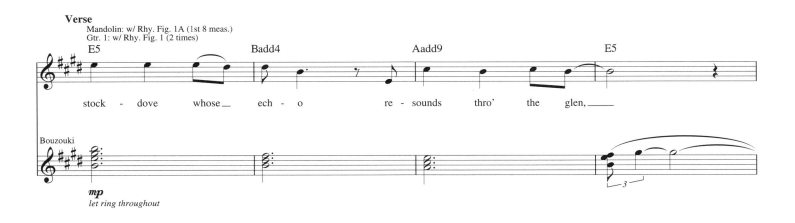

stock - dove whose __ ech - o re - sounds thro' the glen, __

oh, ye wild __ whist - ling black - birds in

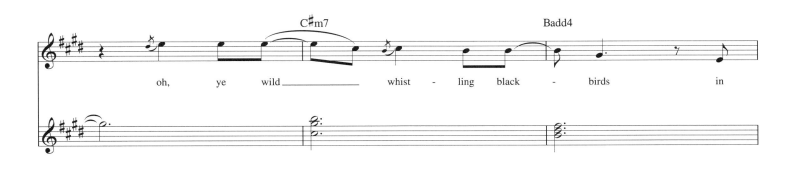

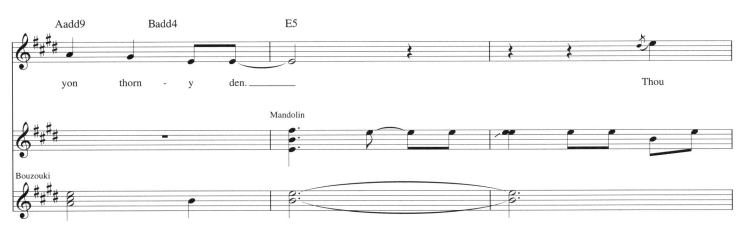

yon thorn - y den. __ Thou

Bridge

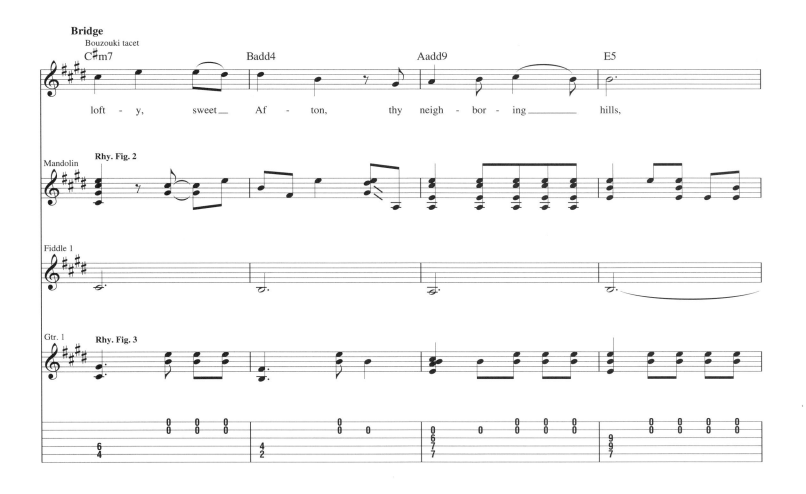

loft - y, sweet_ Af - ton, thy neigh - bor - ing_____ hills,

far mark'd with the cours - es of clear wind - ing rills._

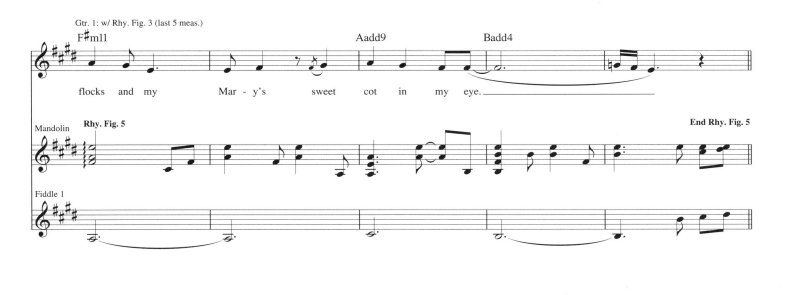

flocks and my Mar - y's sweet cot in my eye.

Interlude

Fiddle 1: w/ Riff B (1st 8 meas.)
Mandolin: w/ Riff A
Gtr. 1: w/ Rhy. Fig. 1 (2 times)

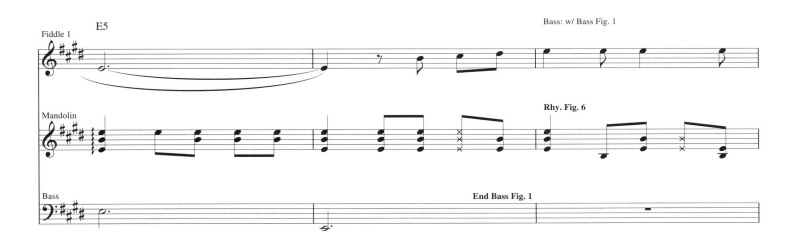

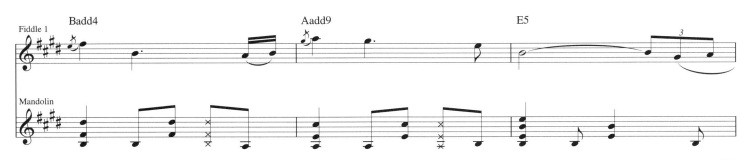

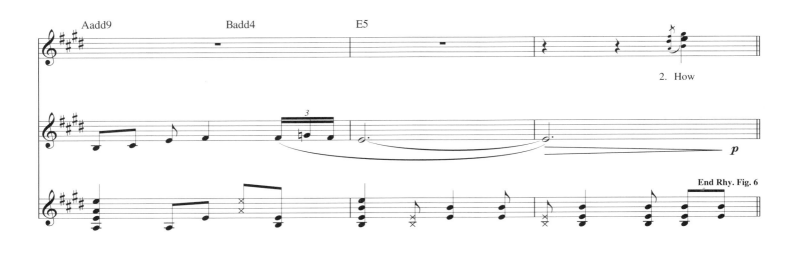

Verse

Fiddle 1 tacet
Mandolin: w/ Rhy. Fig. 6 (2 times)
Gtr. 1: w/ Rhy. Fig. 1 (2 times)
Bass: w/ Bass Fig. 1 (2 times)

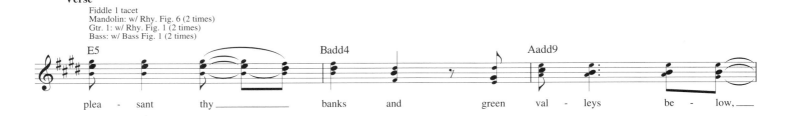

plea - sant thy _____ banks and green val - leys be - low, ____

_____ where wild in the wood -

- lands the prim - ros - es blow. _____ There

oft as mild ev' - ning sweeps o - ver the lea, ___

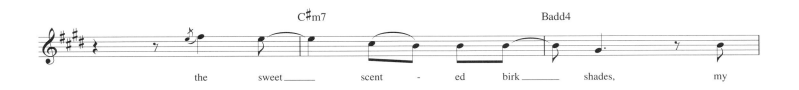

the sweet ___ scent - ed birk ___ shades, my

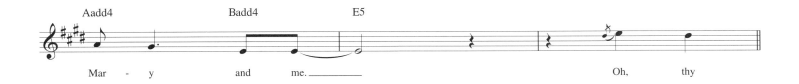

Mar - y and me. ___ Oh, thy

Bridge

Mandolin: w/ Rhy. Fig. 2
Gtr. 1: w/ Rhy. Fig. 3

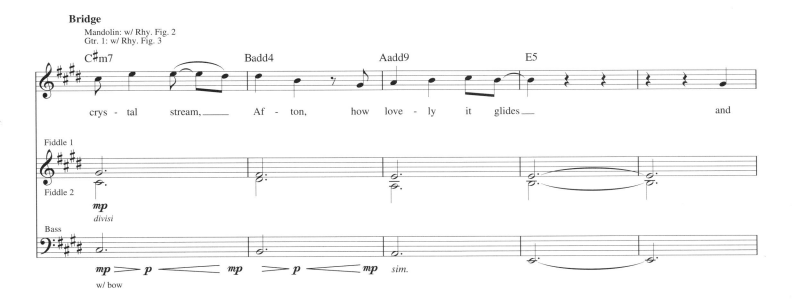

crys - tal stream, ___ Af - ton, how love - ly it glides ___ and

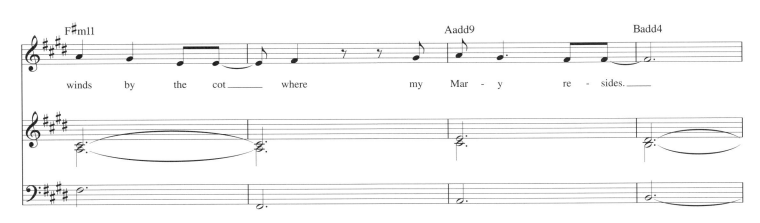

winds by the cot ___ where my Mar - y re - sides. ___

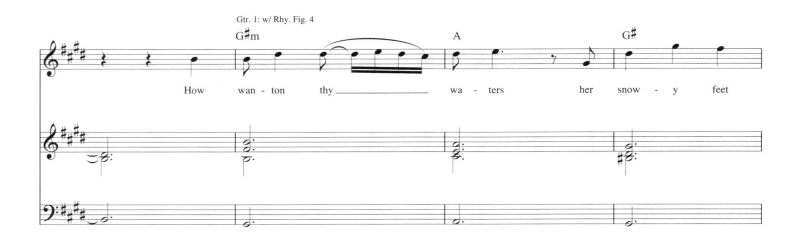

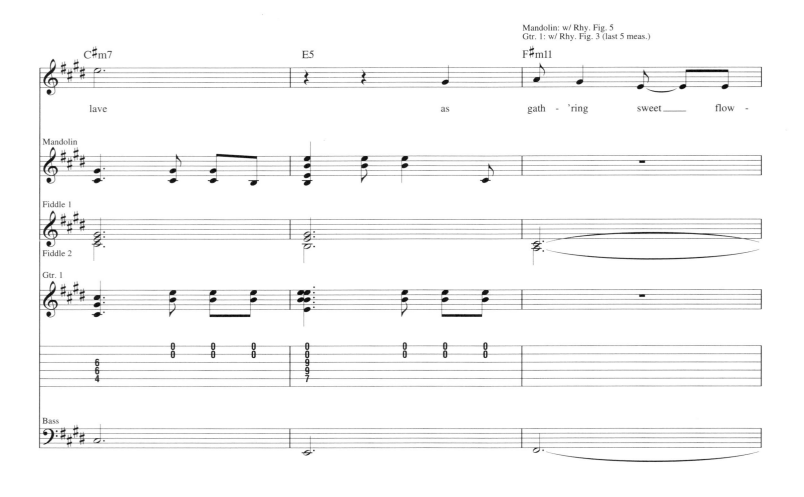

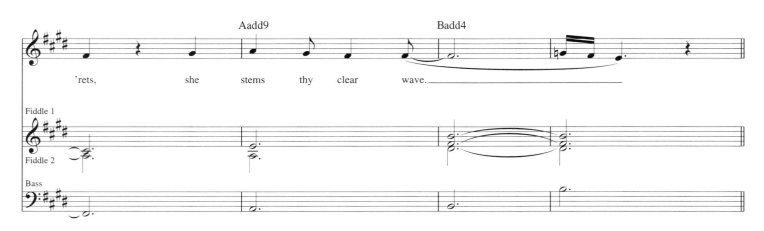

Interlude

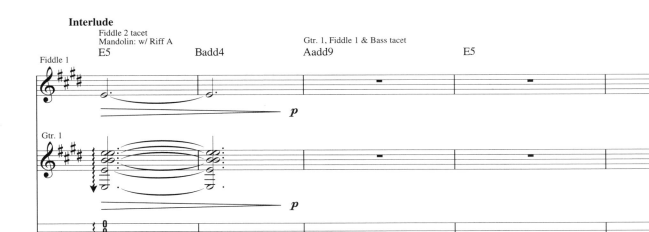

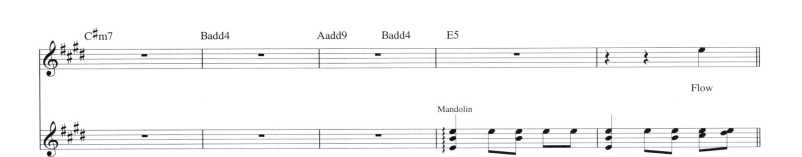

Outro-Chorus

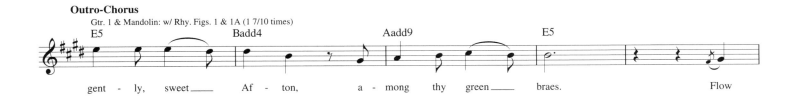

gent - ly, sweet___ Af - ton, a - mong thy green___ braes. Flow

gent - ly, sweet___ riv - er,___ the theme of my lays.

My Mar - y's a - sleep___ by thy mur - mur - ing___ stream.

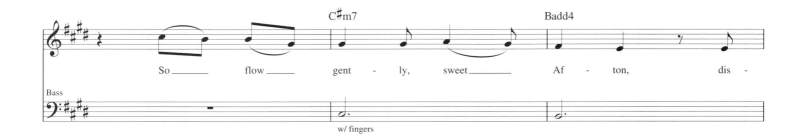

So ___ flow ___ gent - ly, sweet ___ Af - ton, dis-

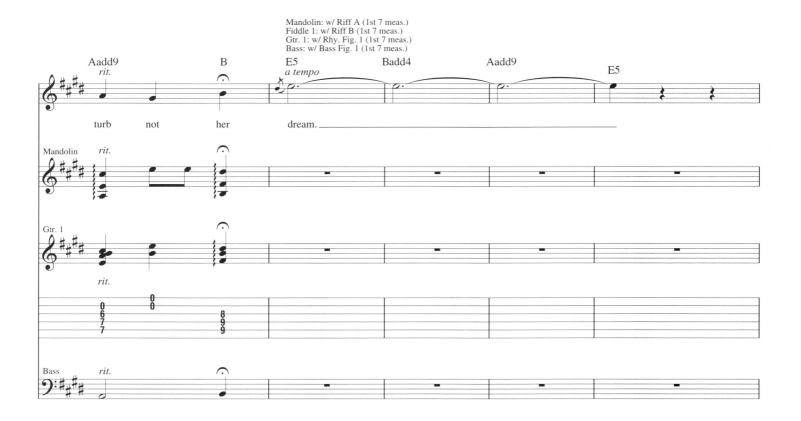

Mandolin: w/ Riff A (1st 7 meas.)
Fiddle 1: w/ Riff B (1st 7 meas.)
Gtr. 1: w/ Rhy. Fig. 1 (1st 7 meas.)
Bass: w/ Bass Fig. 1 (1st 7 meas.)

turb ___ not ___ her ___ dream. _____

Cuckoo's Nest

Traditional

Gtr. 1: Drop D tuning:
(low to high) D-A-D-G-B-E
Bouzouki tuning:
(low to high) G-D-A-E

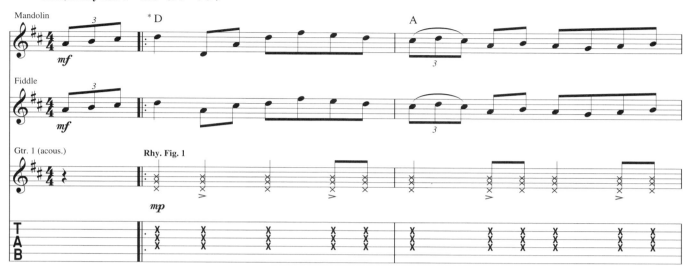

* Chord symbols reflect implied harmony.

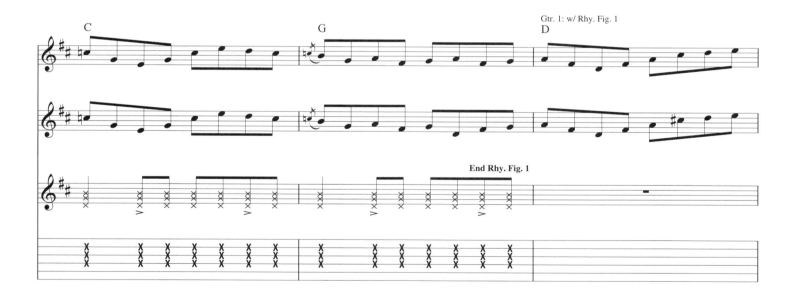

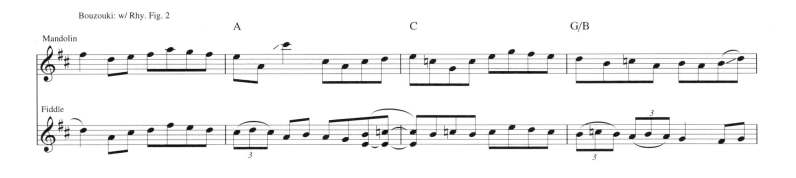

D

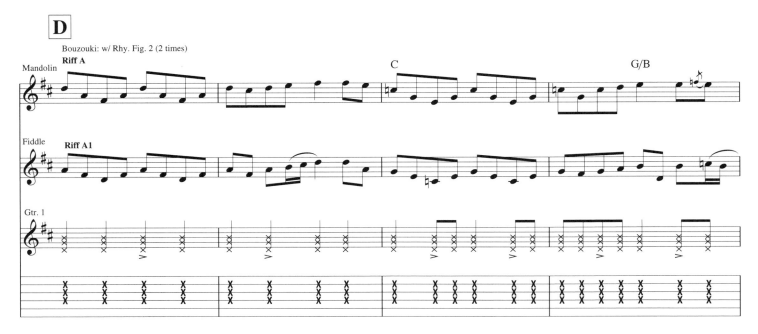

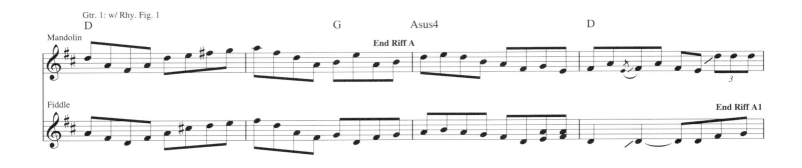

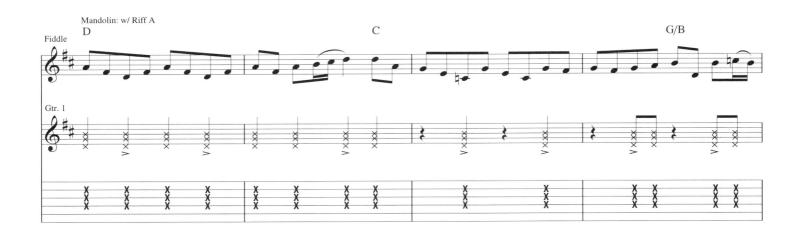

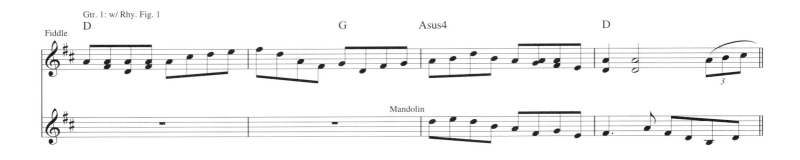

E

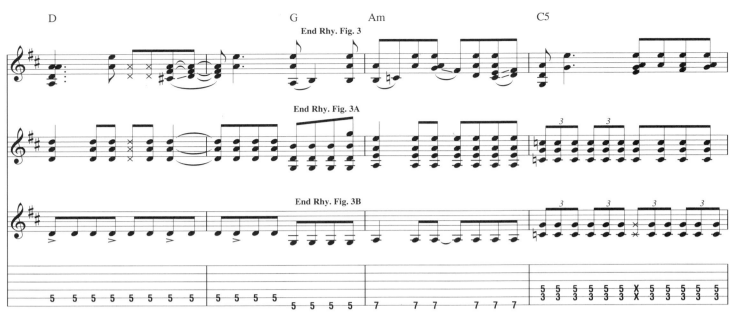

The Hand Song

Words and Music by Sean Watkins and David Puckett

Gtr.1: Capo IV

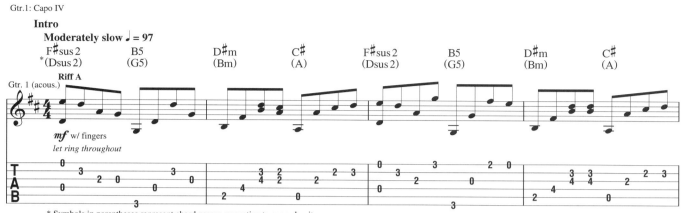

* Symbols in parentheses represent chord names respective to capoed guitar.
Symbols above reflect actual sounding chords. Capoed fret is "0" in tab.

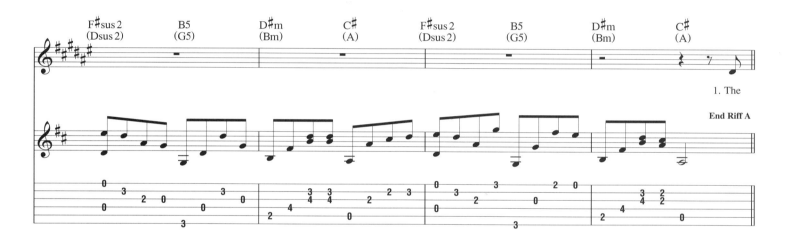

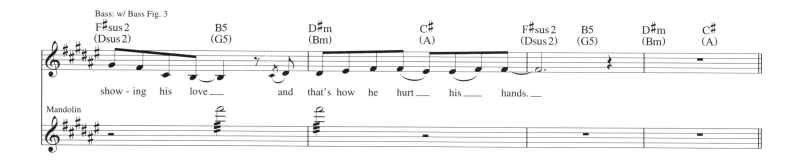

Verse

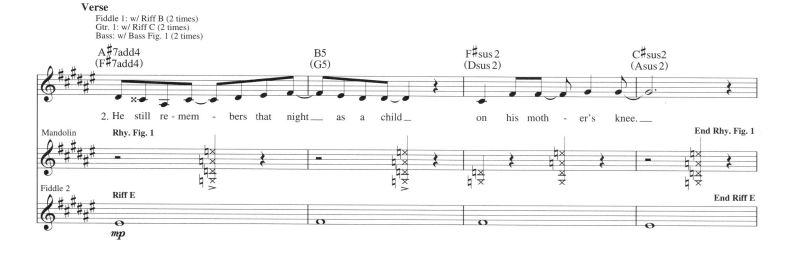

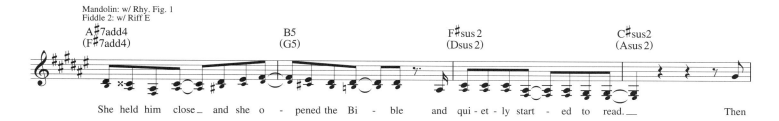

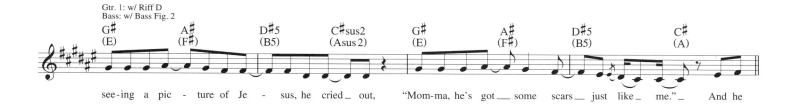

Chorus

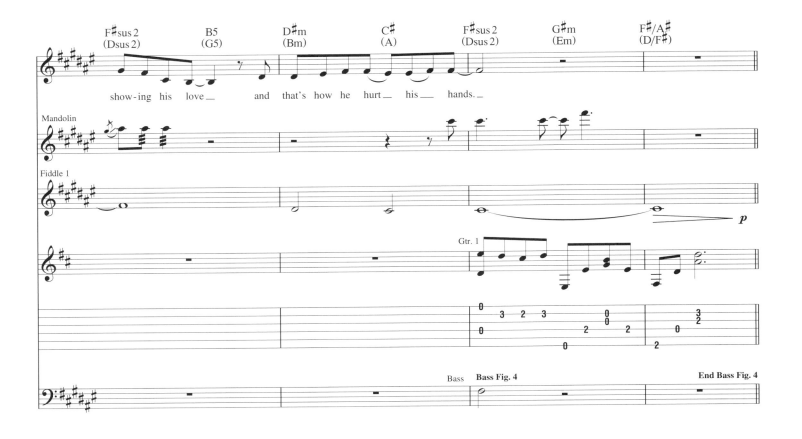

show-ing his love __ and that's how he hurt __ his __ hands. __

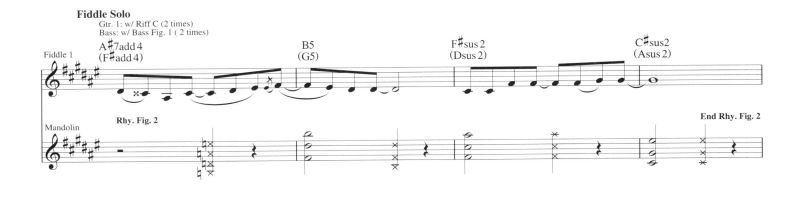

Interlude

Fiddles 1 & 2 tacet
Bass: w/ Bass Fig. 3 (1st 2 meas.)

Bass: w/ Bass Fig. 4

Verse

Mandolin: w/ Rhy. Fig. 2 (2 times)
Gtr. 1: w/ Riff C (2 times)
Bass: w/ Bass Fig. 1 (2 times)

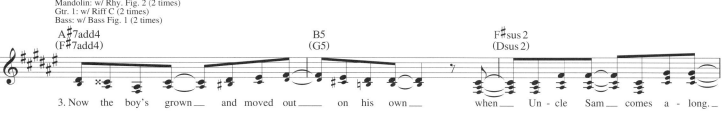

3. Now the boy's grown ___ and moved out ___ on his own ___ when ___ Un - cle Sam ___ comes a - long. ___

A for - eign af - fair, ___ but our young ___ men were there ___ and

Mandolin: w/ Rhy. Fig. 1
Gtr. 1 & Fiddle 1: w/ Riffs D & D1
Bass: w/ Bass Fig. 2

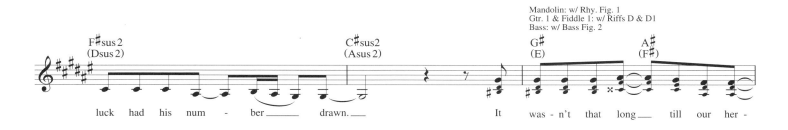

luck had his num - ber ___ drawn. ___ It was - n't that long ___ till our her -

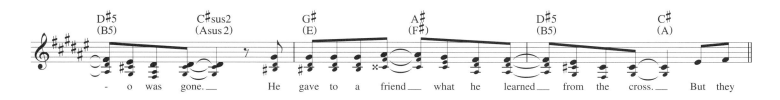

- o was gone. ___ He gave to a friend ___ what he learned ___ from the cross. ___ But they

Chorus

Gtr. 1: w/ Riff A (1st 7 meas.)
Bass: w/ Bass Fig. 3 (3 1/2 times)

knew it was love, ___ it was one they could un - der - stand. ___ He was

Robin and Marian

Words and Music by Sean Watkins

*Composite arrangement.

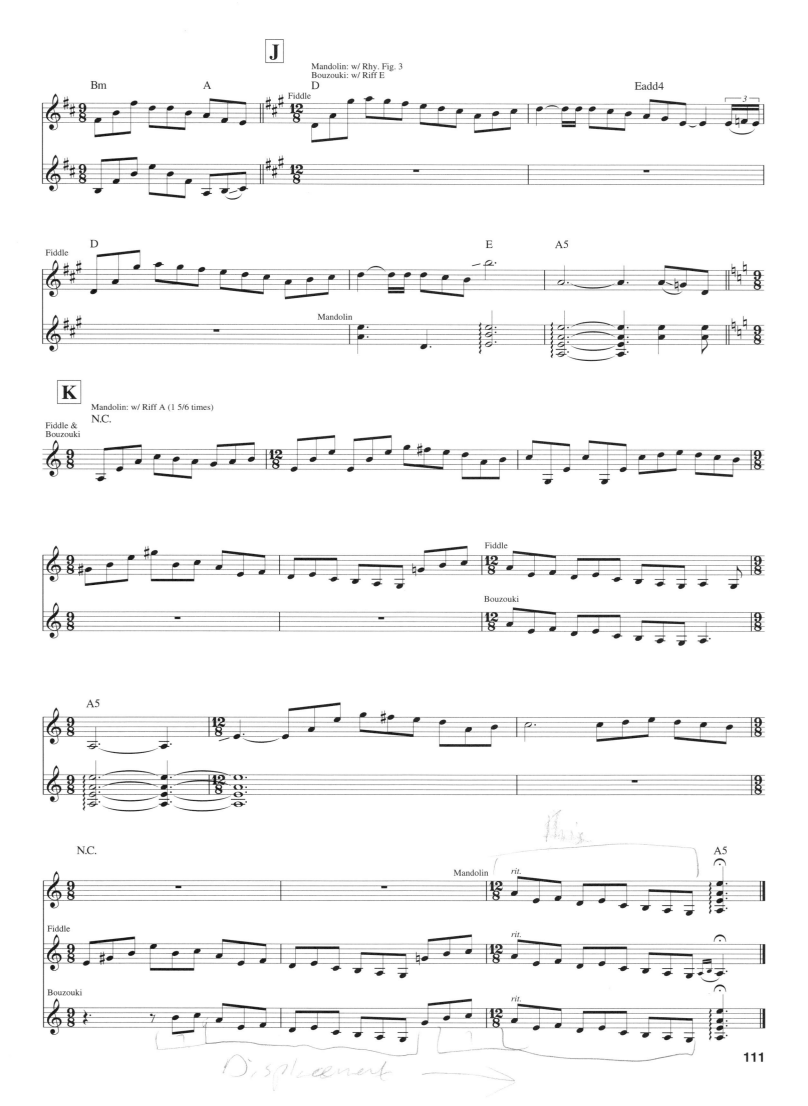

The Fox

Traditional
Arranged by Chris Thile, Sean Watkins and Sara Watkins

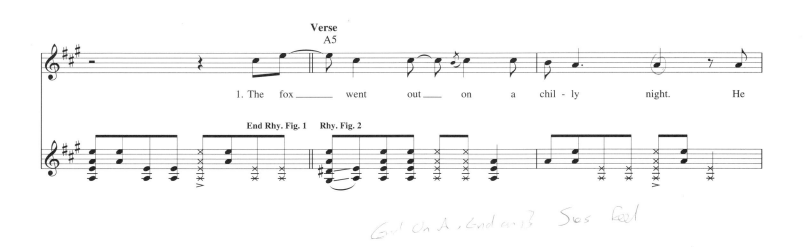

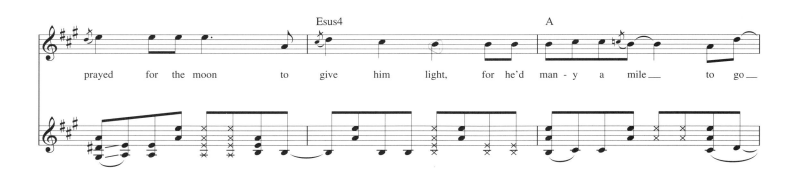

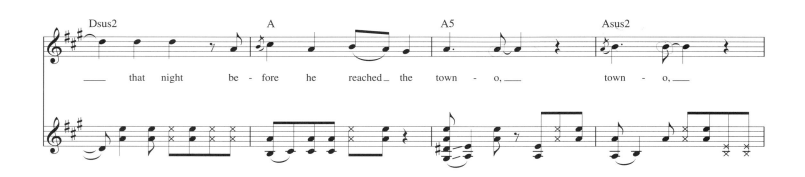

town - o. ___ He'd man-y a mile ___ to go that night be-fore ___ he reached ___ the

End Rhy. Fig. 2

Mandolin: w/ Rhy. Fig. 1

town - o. _____

2. He ___

Gtr. 1 (acous.)

mf

let ring throughout

* Symbols in parentheses represent chord names respective to capoed guitar.
Symbols above reflect actual sounding chords. Capoed fret is "0" in tab.

Verse

Mandolin: w/ Rhy. Fig. 2

ran till he came to the farm - er's pen. The ducks and the geese were kept ___

___ there - in. ___ He said, "A cou - ple of you ___ are gon - na grease my chin be -

End half-time feel

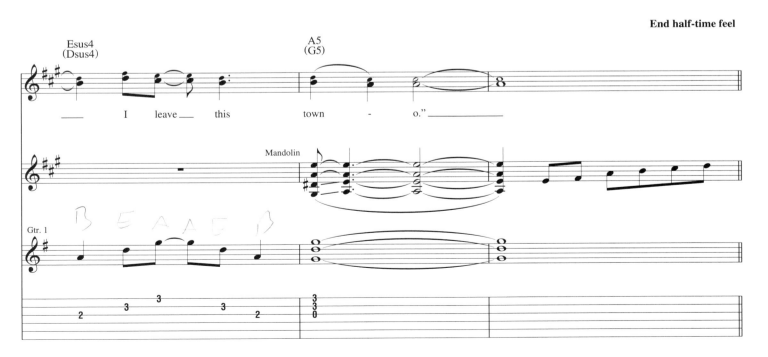

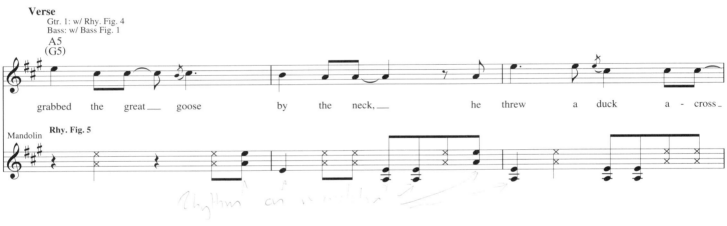

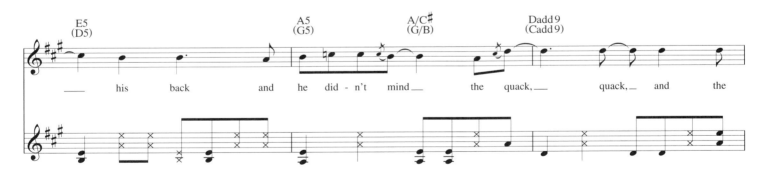

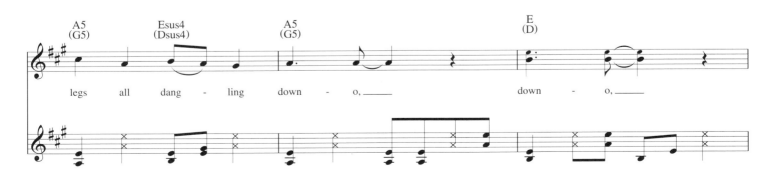

Outro
Gtr. 1: w/ Rhy. Fig. 4 (1st 13 meas.)
Bass: w/ Bass Fig. 1 (1st 13 meas.)

Pastures New

Words and Music by Sean Watkins

*Chord symbols reflect implied harmony.

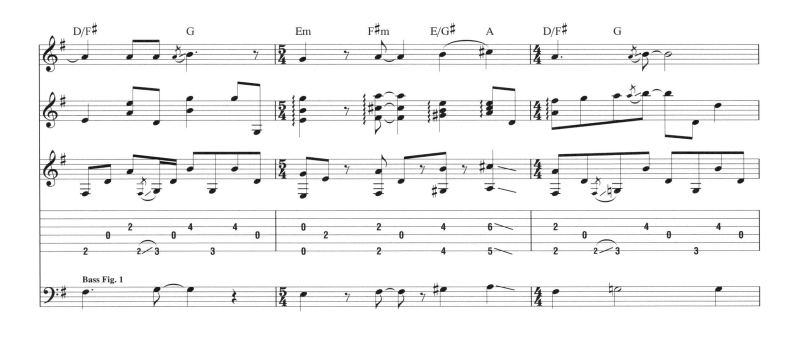

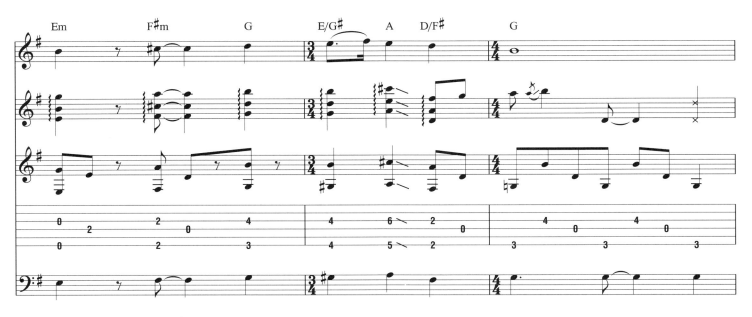

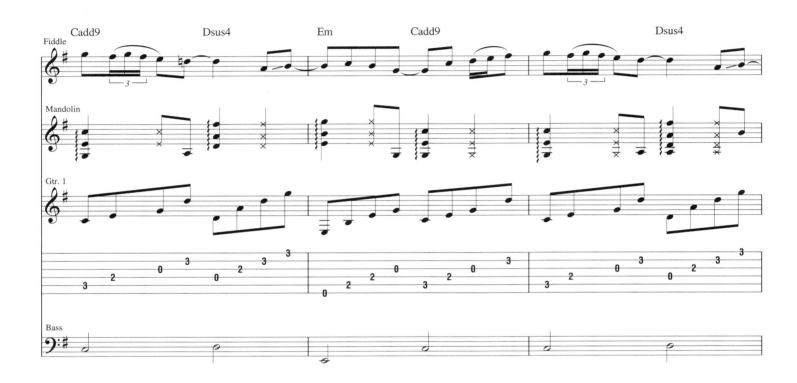

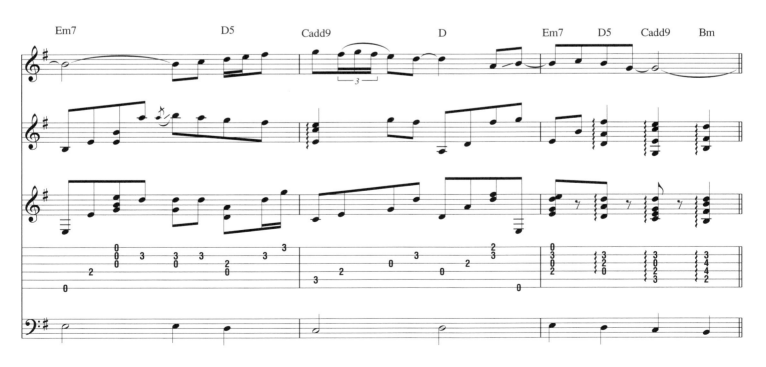

RECORDED VERSIONS
The Best Note-For-Note Transcriptions Available

RECORDED VERSIONS GUITAR

ALL BOOKS INCLUDE TABLATURE

00690501	Adams, Bryan – Greatest Hits	$19.95
00692015	Aerosmith – Greatest Hits	$22.95
00690488	Aerosmith – Just Push Play	$19.95
00690178	Alice in Chains – Acoustic	$19.95
00690387	Alice in Chains – Nothing Safe – The Best of the Box	$19.95
00694932	Allman Brothers Band – Volume 1	$24.95
00694933	Allman Brothers Band – Volume 2	$24.95
00690513	American Hi-Fi	$19.95
00694878	Atkins, Chet – Vintage Fingerstyle	$19.95
00690418	Audio Adrenaline, Best of	$17.95
00690366	Bad Company Original Anthology - Bk 1	$19.95
00690367	Bad Company Original Anthology - Bk 2	$19.95
00690503	Beach Boys – Very Best of	$19.95
00690489	Beatles – 1	$24.95
00694929	Beatles – 1962-1966	$24.95
00694930	Beatles – 1967-1970	$24.95
00694832	Beatles – For Acoustic Guitar	$19.95
00690503	Beatles – Hard Day's Night	$16.95
00690482	Beatles – Let It Be	$16.95
00694884	Benson, George – Best of	$19.95
00692385	Berry, Chuck	$19.95
00692200	Black Sabbath – We Sold Our Soul for Rock 'N' Roll	$19.95
00690305	Blink 182 – Dude Ranch	$19.95
00690389	Blink 182 – Enema of the State	$19.95
00690523	Blink 182 – Take Off Your Pants & Jacket	$19.95
00690028	Blue Oyster Cult – Cult Classics	$19.95
00690583	Boxcar Racer	$19.95
00690491	Bowie, David – Best of	$19.95
00690451	Buckley, Jeff – Collection	$24.95
00690364	Cake – Songbook	$19.95
00690565	Calling, The – Camino Palmero	$29.95
00690293	Chapman, Steven Curtis – Best of	$19.95
00690043	Cheap Trick – Best of	$19.95
00690171	Chicago – Definitive Guitar Collection	$22.95
00690590	Clapton, Eric – Anthology	$29.95
00692931	Clapton, Eric – Best of, 2nd Edition	$22.95
00690415	Clapton Chronicles – Best of Eric Clapton	$18.95
00690074	Clapton, Eric – The Cream of Clapton	$24.95
00694869	Clapton, Eric – Unplugged	$22.95
00690162	Clash, Best of The	$19.95
00690494	Coldplay – Parachutes	$19.95
00690593	Coldplay – A Rush of Blood to the Head	$19.95
00690306	Coryell, Larry – Collection	$19.95
00694940	Counting Crows – August & Everything After	$19.95
00694840	Cream – Disraeli Gears	$19.95
00690401	Creed – Human Clay	$19.95
00690352	Creed – My Own Prison	$19.95
00690551	Creed – Weathered	$19.95
00699521	Cure, The	$24.95
00690484	dc Talk – Intermission: The Greatest Hits	$19.95
00690289	Deep Purple, Best of	$17.95
00690563	Default – The Fallout	$19.95
00690384	Di Franco, Ani – Best of	$19.95
00690380	Di Franco, Ani – Up Up Up Up Up Up	$19.95
00695382	Dire Straits – Sultans of Swing	$19.95
00690347	Doors, The – Anthology	$22.95
00690348	Doors, The – Essential Guitar Collection	$16.95
00690533	Electric Light Orchestra Guitar Collection	$19.95
00690555	Etheridge, Melissa – Best of	$19.95
00690524	Etheridge, Melissa – Skin	$19.95
00690349	Eve 6	$19.95
00690496	Everclear, Best of	$19.95
00690515	Extreme II – Pornograffitti	$19.95
00690323	Fastball – All the Pain Money Can Buy	$19.95
00690235	Foo Fighters – The Colour and the Shape	$19.95
00690394	Foo Fighters – There Is Nothing Left to Lose	$19.95
00690222	G3 Live – Satriani, Vai, Johnson	$22.95
00690536	Garbage – Beautiful Garbage	$19.95
00690438	Genesis Guitar Anthology	$19.95
00690338	Goo Goo Dolls – Dizzy Up the Girl	$19.95
00690576	Goo Goo Dolls – Gutterflower	$19.95
00690114	Guy, Buddy – Collection Vol. A-J	$22.95
00690193	Guy, Buddy – Collection Vol. L-Y	$22.95
00694798	Harrison, George – Anthology	$19.95
00692930	Hendrix, Jimi – Are You Experienced?	$24.95
00692931	Hendrix, Jimi – Axis: Bold As Love	$22.95
00690017	Hendrix, Jimi – Woodstock	$24.95
00660029	Holly, Buddy	$19.95
00690457	Incubus – Make Yourself	$19.95
00690544	Incubus – Morningview	$19.95
00690136	Indigo Girls – 1200 Curfews	$22.95
00694833	Joel, Billy – For Guitar	$19.95
00694912	Johnson, Eric – Ah Via Musicom	$19.95
00690271	Johnson, Robert – The New Transcriptions	$24.95
00699131	Joplin, Janis – Best of	$19.95
00693185	Judas Priest – Vintage Hits	$19.95
00690504	King, Albert – The Very Best of	$19.95
00690444	King, B.B. and Eric Clapton – Riding with the King	$19.95
00690339	Kinks, The – Best of	$19.95
00690279	Liebert, Ottmar + Luna Negra – Opium Highlights	$19.95
00690525	Lynch, George – Best of	$19.95
00694755	Malmsteen, Yngwie – Rising Force	$19.95
00694956	Marley, Bob – Legend	$19.95
00690548	Marley, Bob – One Love: Very Best of	$19.95
00694945	Marley, Bob – Songs of Freedom	$24.95
00690382	McLachlan, Sarah – Mirrorball	$19.95
00690239	Matchbox 20 – Yourself or Someone Like You	$19.95
00694952	Megadeth – Countdown to Extinction	$19.95
00694951	Megadeth – Rust in Peace	$22.95
00690505	Megadeth – The World Needs a Hero	$19.95
00690505	Mellencamp, John – Guitar Collection	$19.95
00690448	MxPx – The Ever Passing Moment	$19.95
00690500	Nelson, Ricky – Guitar Collection	$17.95
00690189	Nirvana – From the Muddy Banks of the Wishkah	$19.95
00694913	Nirvana – In Utero	$19.95
00694883	Nirvana – Nevermind™	$19.95
00690026	Nirvana – Unplugged in New York	$19.95
00690121	Oasis – (What's the Story) Morning Glory	$19.95
00690358	Offspring, The – Americana	$19.95
00690485	Offspring, The – Conspiracy of One	$19.95
00690552	Offspring, The – Ignition	$19.95
00694847	Osbourne, Ozzy – Best of	$22.95
00690547	Osbourne, Ozzy – Down to Earth	$19.95
00690399	Osbourne, Ozzy – Ozzman Cometh	$19.95
00690538	Oysterhead – The Grand Pecking Order	$19.95
00694855	Pearl Jam – Ten	$19.95
00690439	Perfect Circle, A – Mer De Noms	$19.95
00690499	Petty, Tom – The Definitive Guitar Collection	$19.95
00690424	Phish – Farmhouse	$19.95
00690240	Phish – Hoist	$19.95
00690331	Phish – Story of the Ghost	$19.95
00690428	Pink Floyd – Dark Side of the Moon	$19.95
00690456	P.O.D. – The Fundamental Elements of Southtown	$19.95
00690546	P.O.D. – Satellite	$19.95
00693864	Police, The – Best of	$19.95
00690299	Presley, Elvis – Best of Elvis: The King of Rock 'n' Roll	$19.95
00694975	Queen – Greatest Hits	$24.95
00694910	Rage Against the Machine	$19.95
00690145	Rage Against the Machine – Evil Empire	$19.95
00690478	Rage Against the Machine – Renegades	$19.95
00690426	Ratt – Best of	$19.95
00690055	Red Hot Chili Peppers – Bloodsugarsexmagik	$19.95
00690584	Red Hot Chili Peppers – By the Way	$19.95
00690379	Red Hot Chili Peppers – Californication	$19.95
00690090	Red Hot Chili Peppers – One Hot Minute	$22.95
00694899	R.E.M. – Automatic for the People	$19.95
00690511	Reinhardt, Django – Definitive Collection	$19.95
00690014	Rolling Stones – Exile on Main Street	$24.95
00690031	Santana's Greatest Hits	$19.95
00690566	Scorpions – Best of	$19.95
00120123	Shepherd, Kenny Wayne – Trouble Is	$19.95
00690419	Slipknot	$19.95
00690530	Slipknot – Iowa	$19.95
00690385	Sonicflood	$19.95
00694957	Stewart, Rod – Unplugged...And Seated	$22.95
00690021	Sting – Fields of Gold	$19.95
00690520	Styx Guitar Collection	$19.95
00690519	Sum 41 – All Killer No Filler	$19.95
00690425	System of a Down	$19.95
00690531	System of a Down – Toxicity	$19.95
00694824	Taylor, James – Best of	$16.95
00690238	Third Eye Blind	$19.95
00690580	311 – From Chaos	$19.95
00690295	Tool – Aenima	$19.95
00690039	Vai, Steve – Alien Love Secrets	$24.95
00690343	Vai, Steve – Flex-able Leftovers	$19.95
00690392	Vai, Steve – The Ultra Zone	$19.95
00690370	Vaughan, Stevie Ray and Double Trouble – The Real Deal: Greatest Hits Volume 2	$22.95
00690116	Vaughan, Stevie Ray – Guitar Collection	$24.95
00660058	Vaughan, Stevie Ray – Lightnin' Blues 1983-1987	$24.95
00690550	Vaughan, Stevie Ray and Double Trouble – Live at Montreux 1982 & 1985	$24.95
00694835	Vaughan, Stevie Ray – The Sky Is Crying	$22.95
00690015	Vaughan, Stevie Ray – Texas Flood	$19.95
00694789	Waters, Muddy – Deep Blues	$24.95
00690071	Weezer (The Blue Album)	$19.95
00690516	Weezer (The Green Album)	$19.95
00690579	Weezer – Maladroit	$19.95
00690286	Weezer – Pinkerton	$19.95
00690447	Who, The – Best of	$24.95
00690320	Williams, Dar – Best of	$17.95
00690319	Wonder, Stevie – Some of the Best	$17.95
00690443	Zappa, Frank – Hot Rats	$19.95
00690589	ZZ Top Guitar Anthology	$22.95